THE **POLITICAL PLATFORM** OF
THE LORD AND KING

by Galyn Wiemers

Last Hope Books and Publications
A Division of Generation Word Bible Teaching Ministry

The Political Platform of the Lord and King
Copyright 2010 by Galyn Wiemers. All Rights reserved.
Printed in the United States of America by
Signature Book Printing. www.sbpbooks.com

Last Hope Books and Publications
A Division of Generation Word Bible Teaching Ministry
P.O. Box 399
Waukee, Iowa 50263

Visit www.generationword.com

All scripture passages are from the New International Version

Cover design by Clint Hansen
Editing by Jennifer Ruisch and Tim Vaniman
Back cover photo by Toni Wiemers

ISBN- 13: 978-0-9794382-2-6
ISBN- 10: 0-9794382-2-5

This book is dedicated to the United Nations, national leaders and politicians.

Be warned, you rulers of the earth.
- King David, 1000 BC, Psalm 2:10

In the time of those kings, the God of heaven will set up a kingdom that will never be destroyed, nor will it be left to another people. It will crush all those kingdoms and bring them to an end, but it will itself endure forever.
- Daniel, 604 BC, Daniel 2:44

This gospel of the kingdom will be preached in the whole world as a testimony to all nations, and then the end will come.
- Jesus, 30 AD, Matthew 24:14

The kingdom of the world has become the kingdom of our Lord and of his Christ, and he will reign for ever and ever.
- John, 96 AD, Revelation 11:15

Introduction	6
Chapter 1 **The Mount of Olives Scenario**	8
Chapter 2 **The Ultimate Foreign Invasion**	12
Chapter 3 **The Decline of Authority**	22
Chapter 4 **The Policies of the Lord's Administration**	28
Chapter 5 **The Final Battle**	48
Chapter 6 **The Transfer of the Empire**	52
Chapter 7 **Meeting the Lord and King Today**	55

Introduction

In an age that is filled with conflicting opinions and societies in turmoil, we must realize it has always been this way. There was never a time that all sides agreed to which battle strategy was correct, who the enemy was, which laws should be enforced, what role government has in demanding service from or providing service for their citizens, or how to treat the land, the people, the money, the businesses, the religion(s) or the next generation.

Egyptians did not all agree with Egypt. A new pharaoh would often overturn the previous pharaoh's policies, even defacing their monuments. Greece was so divided that it took the approaching Persian Empire to finally clarify who the real enemy was. Even then, many Greeks considered the Persian Empire an opportunity and not an opponent. After Alexander the Great died, his generals spent the next generations warring with each other in an attempt to rebuild the lost unity of the empire. When was Rome not at war? And, when did the Romans (emperor, senate and people) ever agree on any Roman policy? So it continues today with issues such as education, energy, immigration, health care, housing, environment, big business, small business, military, capital punishment, crime, taxation, Israel . . .

Even knowing that this is the way the world works we still find ourselves wanting unity. We want to agree. We want to hear people voice opinions that we already accept, or at least can understand and learn to accept. We find ourselves listening, talking and hoping that after civilized debate and a reasonable amount of time, everyone will recognize the truth and we will emerge as a unified culture. One voice, one opinion, one nation undivided! But, it has not happened. Nor, do I think, can it.

As we live our lives and make our way through time in this dark, divided, drifting world, we still seek light, unity and direction from the truth. But we ask, as did the Roman governor Pontius Pilate, "What is truth?" Is truth what I think? Is truth what you think? Is truth what they think? Is truth a selected combination of what we all think? Is truth everything everybody thinks? Then today especially we ask, "Is there truth?" Is there even a reason for looking for truth at all?

Although, I do not think we will ever find complete unity on this side of history, I do believe that truth exists. I do not think everyone will find it, because I don't believe everybody has the ability, desire or heart to do so. But I do believe truth exists and is available to us today. So how do we find it? And then how can we take that truth and write it into a political platform that we can present to the people? This has been a source of frustration, even anger and disillusionment, for me. The more we talk and teach, the more committed we become to what we believe. This only seems to widen the divide. How can we navigate through our cultural issues?

To find the perfect political platform I decided to go to the Bible and read the end of the story. In the end, there will be a perfect culture administrated by a perfect man. He will be the judge, lawgiver and king (the judicial, legislative and executive branch all in one, Isaiah 33:22). He will be both the teacher and the king (a dictator, if you can accept that term - Zechariah 14:9). He will be the militant peacekeeper, Jesus Christ.

I am not sure how useful this book will be in helping form contemporary political policy. But I do think it can encourage those of us engaged in the battle to find, reveal and teach truth. Simply knowing the ultimate future can be an encouragement in itself on our journey to pursue the truth. Hopefully this book will be a source of hope for a disillusioned and discouraged culture that appears to be fading into an abyss of chaos. It is already a source of hope for me as I write these thoughts. I write this as an encouragement to you to wait faithfully and expectantly for our Lord Jesus Christ. May his kingdom come and his will be done on earth as it is in heaven.

That last sentence may sound like a ritual recitation of a religious church reading on a lazy Sunday morning or a phrase uttered in thoughtless unison at a graveside service, but it is the most militant statement of loyalty to a foreign regime ever uttered by human lips.

> *"YOUR KINGDOM COME, YOUR WILL BE DONE ON EARTH AS IT IS IN HEAVEN"*
> (Jesus teaching his disciples how to pray in Matthew 6:10)

This prayer, this oath of commitment, is the battle cry of a heart seeking to hand the kingdoms of this world over to the Lord and King. And, this prayer will be answered.

Here is a description of the political platform of the Lord and King, Jesus Christ.

> *The God of heaven will set up a kingdom that will never be destroyed, nor will it be left to another people. It will crush all those kingdoms and bring them to an end, but it will itself endure forever.* –Daniel 2:44, 45

> *For the Lord is our judge, the Lord is our lawgiver, the Lord is our king, it is he who will save us.* –Isaiah 33:22

Chapter One
The Mount of Olives Scenario

Just outside the city walls of Jerusalem in 30 AD, Jesus stood to the east on the Mount of Olives with his disciples. Forty-three days earlier Jesus had been crucified on a cross by the Romans and then raised from the dead three days later. Now, forty days after his resurrection, Jesus stood with his disciples who asked:

> *Lord, are you at this time going to restore the kingdom to Israel?*
> –Acts 1:17

The disciples were asking this question because the Old Testament often spoke of Israel's restoration and their coming Messiah, or king, who would rule the world. These same scriptures foretold physical details of events that had occurred while these disciples were alive. According to the Old Testament, the Messiah would come through the family of Abraham (Genesis 12:3; 18:18) from the tribe of Judah (Genesis 49:10) in the royal line of King David (Psalm 132:11; Jeremiah 23:5-6; 33:15-16). The scriptures spoke of his birth in Bethlehem (Micah 5:2), his residence in Galilee (Isaiah 9:1-7) and his ministry of teaching (Psalm 78:2) and healing (Isaiah 35:5-6). The prophets wrote in great detail about his physical death by crucifixion (Isaiah 53:5-9) including a description of his pierced hands and feet (Psalm 22:16), men gambling for his clothing (Psalm 22:18), his unbroken bones (Psalm 22:17; 34:20), the beverage of vinegar and gall given to him (Psalm 69:21), how he was beaten, mocked and spat upon (Isaiah 50:6), crucified alongside criminals (53:12), buried with the rich (Isaiah 53:9), accused by false witnesses (Psalm 35:11) and betrayed by a friend (Psalm 41:9) for thirty pieces of silver (Zechariah 11:12-13). Even his appearance on a donkey (Zechariah 9:9) was scheduled beforehand, with the specific time revealed in scripture (Daniel 9:25-26).

After seeing all these prophecies fulfilled in a 38-month stretch of time, the disciples had a right to ask, "What about the rest of the prophecies? Are they going to be fulfilled now?" I assume they expected a positive answer; and although Jesus' response is not a rousing affirmative, nor is it resoundingly negative. Instead, Jesus responds with an answer that has two basic parts that can be summarized as, "Yes, but not now. First, there is something we must do."

When the disciples asked, "Are you at this time going to restore the kingdom to Israel?" Jesus replied:

> *It is not for you to know the times or dates the Father has set by his own authority. But, you will receive power when the Holy Spirit comes on you; and you will be my witnesses in Jerusalem, and in all Judea and Samaria, and to the ends of the earth.* –Acts 1:7-8

Basically Jesus told them that the answer was above their pay grade and rank. The first part of his statement left the answer in the realm of mystery, but with an affirmative connection to a future day. The second part of his response identified both the source of power and the initiating event that would usher in the next phase of the kingdom's work in time – the church age.

> *After he said this, he was taken up before their very eyes and a cloud hid him from their sight.* –Acts 1:9

After Jesus' response concerning the restoration of Israel and the institution of the church age, he physically rose into the air until he reached the clouds. The disciples witnessed this event with their own eyes. It was not some kind of spiritual vision; it was a physical event that took place on the Mount of Olives in 30 AD. The mention of "clouds" is important since Jesus had testified 43 days earlier before the high priest of Israel:

> *In the future you will see the Son of Man sitting at the right hand of the Mighty One and coming on the clouds of heaven.* –Matthew 26:64

Jesus' reference to his own return to earth "on the clouds of heaven" is a reference to the writings of the prophet Daniel who recorded a vision of a future day when he said:

> *I looked and there before me was one like a son of man, coming with the clouds of heaven. He approached the Ancient of Days and was led into his presence. He was given authority, glory and sovereign power; all peoples, nations and men of every language worshiped him. His dominion is an everlasting dominion that will not pass away, and his kingdom is one that will never be destroyed.* –Daniel 7:13-14

When Jesus spoke to the high priest he was testifying that he himself was the man who would rule as God on the earth in a kingdom that would never be destroyed. In this kingdom Jesus would receive universal worship from every nation in every language. Jesus' ascension into the clouds in 30 AD on the Mount of Olives is a clear indication that he was not going to establish universal dominion at that time. Yet his answer to the disciples' question drew their attention back to Daniel 7:13—confirming the idea that he was saying, "wait." The promises of the Old Testament remained. One like a son of man would appear in the clouds and establish everlasting dominion. But not now.

The details of this event continue in Acts 1:10:

> *They (the disciples) were looking intently up into the sky as he was going, when suddenly two men dressed in white stood beside them. "Men of Galilee," they said, "why do you stand here looking into the sky? This same Jesus, who has been taken from you into heaven, will come back in the same way you have seen him go into heaven."* –Acts 1:10-11

Chapter 1 The Mount of Olives Scenario

Two angels helped explain the event and clarify the timing. Indeed, Jesus would restore Israel and establish his kingdom, but not now. The "men of Galilee," or the disciples, had been told that Jesus would return "the same way" they saw him leave. In the meantime, they were to be witnesses, empowered by the Holy Spirit, taking his message to the ends of the earth. Thus, the angels ask, "Why do you stand here looking into the sky?" It is not going to speed things up! And, looking into the sky waiting for Jesus or wondering when he is going to return is not going to get the new assignment done. The disciples were not told "stand and stare" at the sky from the Mount of Olives, they were told to "go."

When the angels testify that Jesus will return to the Mount of Olives "the same way" he left they draw attention to Zechariah 14:1-9, which was written around 500 BC. The passage speaks of Jerusalem being overthrown while its citizens are slaughtered and taken captive. It is not describing the Assyrian invasion of 701 BC, nor the Babylonian destruction of 586 BC, nor the fall of Jerusalem to the Romans in 70 AD or 135 AD, nor any other battle in Jerusalem since that time. It is describing a battle that is yet to happen.

Zechariah records this:
> A day of the Lord is coming when your plunder will be divided among you. I will gather all the nations to Jerusalem to fight against it; the city will be captured, the houses ransacked, and the women raped. Half of the city will go into exile, but the rest of the people will not be taken from the city. Then the Lord will go out and fight against those nations, as he fights in the day of battle. On that day his feet will stand on the Mount of Olives, east of Jerusalem, and the Mount of Olives will be split in two from east to west, forming a great valley, with half of the mountain moving north and half moving south. You will flee by my mountain valley, for it will extend to Azel. You will flee as you fled from the earthquake in the days of Uzziah king of Judah. Then the Lord my God will come, and all the holy ones with him. On that day there will be no light, no cold or frost. It will be a unique day, without daytime or nighttime— a day known to the Lord. When evening comes, there will be light. On that day living water will flow out from Jerusalem, half to the eastern sea and half to the western sea, in summer and in winter. The Lord will be king over the whole earth. On that day there will be one Lord, and his name the only name. –Zechariah 14:1-9

In this prophecy we see the Lord going out from heaven to engage the nations in battle at Jerusalem. It will not be like the battle in Exodus 14:23-30 when the Egyptian army drowned in the Red Sea, nor like the battle in Judges 4:15 and 5:4, 21 when the storm helped weaken and destroy the Canaanites, nor like the battle in I Samuel 7:10-12 when God rained hailstones on the Philistines. It won't even be like the battle in Isaiah 37:36-37 when the Angel of the Lord struck down 185,000 Assyrian soldiers in one night. On this day the Lord actually leaves heaven (presumably in clouds of glory) and "his feet will stand on the Mount of Olives, east of Jerusalem" just like the two angels stated in Acts 1:11. Just like

Jesus came in a physical body, died in a physical body, was resurrected and ascended in a physical body, this same Jesus will return to earth in a physical body and pick up where he left off—on the Mount of Olives—the same place where his disciples asked him, "Are you at this time going to restore the kingdom to Israel?" Jesus will return to the earth in a physical body to establish a physical kingdom that will have dominion over the earth. Zechariah tells us, "The Lord will be king over the whole earth."

Micah records these same future events like this:

> Now many nations are gathered against you. They say, "Let her be defiled, let our eyes gloat over Zion!" But they do not know the thoughts of the Lord; they do not understand his plan, he who gathers them like sheaves to the threshing floor. Rise and thresh, O Daughter of Zion, for I will give you horns of iron; I will give you hoofs of bronze and you will break to pieces many nations. You will devote their ill-gotten gains to the Lord, their wealth to the Lord of all the earth.
> –Micah 4:11-13

> The Lord says to my Lord:
> "Sit at my right hand until I make your enemies a
> footstool for your feet."
>
> The Lord will extend your mighty scepter from Zion;
> You will rule in the midst of your enemies.
> Your troops will be willing on your day of battle.
> Arrayed in holy majesty, from the womb of the
> dawn you will receive the dew of your youth.
>
> The Lord has sworn and will not change his mind:
> "You are a priest forever, in the order of Melchizedek."
>
> The Lord is at your right hand;
> he will crush kings on the day of his wrath.
> He will judge the nations, heaping up the dead
> and crushing the rulers of the whole earth.
> He will drink from a brook beside the way;
> therefore he will lift up his head. –Psalm 110

Chapter Two
The Ultimate Foreign Invasion

In Acts 1:11 the angels said that, *"This same Jesus, who has been taken from you into heaven, will come back in the same way you have seen him go into heaven."* The angels were speaking of the physical, bodily return of Jesus Christ from heaven to earth just like the disciples had seen his physical ascension from earth to heaven in 30 AD. The angels were not drawing attention to the time of day, the weather, the social climate, the number of people in the crowd or any other surrounding events. The focus was on the man Jesus. He would return to this earth to fulfill all that had been written.

When Jesus returns, it will be a physical, visible return to the Mount of Olives. But, the 2,000 to 3,400-year-old prophecies indicate that what happens after his return is very different. He will set up a kingdom, the likes of which the world has not yet seen. His political platform will be unique, unparalleled on the world scene.

The first issues to discuss concerning the Lord's political platform are:
  A) Military
  B) Defense Budget
  C) Foreign Invasion
  D) Foreign Occupation

The Lord has been portrayed as a humble peacemaker who is willing to overlook grievous offenses. Even his willingness to continue at the negotiating table in the face of declarations of war by humanity has been noted. The abuse of his ambassadors by the world through the ages has caused many to question both his integrity and his willingness to fight fire with fire. Too often this meekness and mercy has been mislabeled as weakness or indifference. But, one of the disciples who was on the Mount of Olives that day in 30 AD said this:

> *The Lord is not slow in keeping his promise, as some understand slowness. He is patient with you, not wanting anyone to perish, but everyone to come to repentance."* –Second Peter 3:9

First we must understand that the Lord is pro-military and supports an extensive military budget. We will see in the following prophecies that the Lord not only uses the military, but that he himself is willing and able to get out in front and lead the troops. He will vigorously engage in the bloodshed of those he confidently calls "the enemy" (also called wicked, evil, etc.). It is hard to imagine today's media allowing him to get away with such a "reckless" and "dangerous" course of action.

Several writers of scripture record the details of the Lord's military policy for us. They make it clear that he is committed to a weapons budget—not a military defense budget, but a military offense budget.

The Political Platform of the Lord and King

In the situation described in Zechariah 14:3 (often called "the second coming"), we see Jesus act out his policy concerning foreign invasion. In the midst of a unified global effort of the nations to overrun Jerusalem (Zechariah 14:2), planet earth is invaded by the Lord. This invasion leads to his military presence and his governmental control for many, many years as he occupies the earth and rules as the king (Zechariah 14:9).

In Zechariah 14:4 Jesus uses the local terrain to his advantage. If the local terrain does not suit his military purposes, he will simply rearrange the surrounding landscape to advance his battle strategy. Upon his arrival, the Mount of Olives is divided in order to form an escape route for the citizens of Jerusalem who are being raped and ransacked by the enemy (Zech. 14:2, 5). The foresight of this topography change is interesting since it will also be the cause of a new waterway that will connect the Mediterranean Sea to the Dead Sea by way of Jerusalem. We will later see Jerusalem become a seaport city during the Lord's dispensation as King of the Earth. The water flowing through Jerusalem will fill the Dead Sea so that the water continues flowing south into the Gulf of Aqaba and on through the Red Sea into the southern ocean, thus connecting the Atlantic and Indian Oceans (Zech.14:8; Ezekiel 47:1-12).

Besides realigning the battlefield for military and eventual reconstruction purposes, the Lord unleashes incredible firepower on his enemies—firepower we must potentially consider to be weapons of mass destruction. Here is Zechariah's account of the release of these incredible weapons financed by the military budget of the Kingdom of our Lord and King:

> This is the plague with which the Lord will strike all the nations that fought against Jerusalem: Their flesh will rot while they are still standing on their feet, their eyes will rot in their sockets, and their tongues will rot in their mouths. . . A similar plague will strike the horses and mules, the camels and donkeys, and all the animals in those camps.
> –Zechariah 14:12, 15

There will be instant death for many in the enemy's camp. Those that do not dissolve where they stand will be struck with such a great panic and fear that they will begin to kill each other.

John, one of the Lord's disciples who stood with him on the Mount of Olives when he ascended in 30 AD, describes the Lord's return like this:

> I saw heaven standing open and there before me was a white horse, whose rider is called Faithful and True. With justice he judges and makes war. His eyes are like blazing fire, and on his head are many crowns. He has a name written on him that no on knows but he himself. He is dressed in a robe dipped in blood, and his name is the Word of God. The armies of heaven were following him, riding on white horses and dressed in fine linen, white and clean. Out of his mouth comes a

Chapter 2 The Ultimate Foreign Invasion

> sharp sword with which to strike down the nations. He will rule them with an iron scepter. He treads the winepress of the fury of the wrath of God Almighty. On his robe and on his thigh he has this name written: KING OF KINGS AND LORD OF LORDS. And I saw an angel standing in the sun, who cried in a loud voice to all the birds flying in midair, "Come, gather together for the great supper of God, so that you may eat the flesh of kings, generals, and mighty men, of horses and their riders, and the flesh of all people, free and slave, small and great". . . The rest of them were killed with the sword that came out of the mouth of the rider on the horse, and all the birds gorged themselves on their flesh. –Revelation 19:11-18, 21

John's recording of an angelic invitation to the birds to feast on the fleshly remains of the enemy that day is alarming. It appears the Lord's political platform has no policy concerning respect for the enemy's dead leaders and troops. This attitude would not be appreciated at the United Nations and would cause serious political hemorrhaging in the polls of the Western world. Yet, the Lord is not concerned with either the UN or the polls.

Isaiah describes this entry battle at the Mount of Olives like this:

> Come near, you nations, and listen; pay attention, you peoples! Let the earth hear, and all that is in it, the world, and all that comes out of it! The Lord is angry with all nations; his wrath is upon all their armies. He will totally destroy them, he will give them over to slaughter. Their slain will be thrown out, their dead bodies will send up a stench; the mountains will be soaked with their blood. –Isaiah 34:1-3

After the Lord's initial invasion of the earth at the Mount of Olives, he turns south to route the enemy and destroy and secure a southern military base. The Edomite (present day southern Jordan) rulers, commanders, military and civilians are portrayed here as sacrificial animals: bulls, bull calves, wild oxen, lambs and goats.

> My sword has drunk its fill in the heavens; see, it descends in judgment on Edom. The people I have totally destroyed. The sword of the Lord is bathed in blood, it is covered with fat—the blood of lambs and goats, fat from the kidneys of rams. For the Lord has a sacrifice in Bozrah and a great slaughter in Edom. And the Wild Oxen will fall with them, the bull, calves and the great bulls. Their land will be drenched with blood and the dust will be soaked with fat. For the Lord has a day of vengeance, a year of retribution to uphold Zion's cause. –Isaiah 34:5-8

Upon the Lord's return from this southern campaign Isaiah catches up with him for an "on-location" interview about this new military phenomenon. Isaiah, like John, draws attention to the Lord's blood stained military garb on that day:

The Political Platform of the Lord and King

> Isaiah: *Who is this coming from Edom, from Bozrah, with his garments stained crimson? Who is this, robed in splendor striding forward in the greatness of his strength?*
>
> Lord: *It is I, speaking in righteousness, mighty to save.*
>
> Isaiah: *Why are your garments red, like those of one treading the winepress?*
>
> Lord: *I have trodden the winepress alone; from the nations no one was with me. I trampled them in my anger and trod them down in my wrath; their blood spattered my garments, and I stained all my clothing. For the day of vengeance was in my heart, and the year of my redemption has come. I looked, but there was no one to help, I was appalled that no one gave support; so my own arm worked salvation for me, and my own wrath sustained me. I trampled the nations in my anger; in my wrath I made them drunk and poured their blood on the ground.*
> –Isaiah 63:1-6

Well, there you have it. In this interview the Lord mentions several times that none of the nations supported his policies, his political platform or his desire to be world leader. He says, "I have trodden the winepress alone" and "no one was with me." He says, "I looked, but there was no one to help" and "I was appalled that no one gave support." The Lord has apparently overthrown the leaders and destroyed the militaries of all the world's nations that still resisted him on the day he returned to the Mount of Olives.

David, the former leader of Israel, warned his fellow world leaders about the Lord's desire to rule the earth. David gave them some good advice concerning this sensitive international predicament.

> David: *Why do the nations conspire and the peoples plot in vain? The kings of the earth take their stand and the rulers gather together against the Lord (God) and against his Anointed One* (Jesus).
>
> Nations (in unison): *Let us break their chains and throw off their fetters.*
>
> The One enthroned in Heaven addressing the nations: (begins with laughing which quickly turns to scoffing, leading to a rebuke of the nations in his anger—a rebuke that terrifies the world leaders and their militaries) *I HAVE INSTALLED MY KING ON ZION, MY HOLY HILL!*
>
> The One enthroned in Heaven addressing Jesus: *You are my Son; today I have become your Father. Ask of me, and I will make the nations your inheritance, and the ends of the earth your possession. You will rule them with an iron scepter; you will dash them to pieces like pottery.*

Chapter 2 The Ultimate Foreign Invasion

> David: *Therefore, you kings, be wise; be warned you rulers of the earth. Serve the Lord* (God) *with fear and rejoice with trembling. Kiss the Son* (Jesus), *lest he be angry and you be destroyed in your way, for his wrath can flare up in a moment.*
>
> David: *Blessed are all who take refuge in him.*—Psalm 2:1-12

Even though all the nations stand against the Lord on the day of his return, both Zechariah and John record that there will be individuals and groups on the earth that join God in battle:

> *On that day men will be stricken by the Lord with great panic. Each man will seize the hand of another, and they will attack each other. Judah too will fight at Jerusalem.* – Zechariah 14:13, 14

The people of Judah living in Jerusalem on that day will be the boots on the ground that will turn to fight with the Lord. Zechariah gives a further description concerning these people of Jerusalem who were waiting for the Lord's return and how they also engage the enemy in battle on that day:

> *On that day, when all the nations of the earth are gathered against her, I will make Jerusalem an immovable rock for all the nations . . . I will keep a watchful eye over the house of Judah, but I will blind all the horses of the nations. Then the leaders of Judah will say in their hearts, "The people of Jerusalem are strong, because the Lord Almighty is their God." On that day I will make the leaders of Judah like a firepot in a woodpile, like a flaming torch among sheaves. They will consume right and left all the surrounding peoples, but Jerusalem will remain intact in her place. The Lord will save the dwellings of Judah first, so that the honor of the house of David and of Jerusalem's inhabitants may not be greater than that of Judah. On that day the Lord will shield those who live in Jerusalem, so that the feeblest among them will be like David, and the house of David will be like God, like the Angel of the Lord going before them. On that day I will set out to destroy all the nations that attack Jerusalem.* –Zechariah 12:3-9

In addition to empowering the Jews and the people of Judah to fight, the Lord does not return from heaven alone (Zechariah 14:5; Jude 14). He has with him the armies of heaven, which of course, include the angelic hosts (Matthew 16:27; 25:31; Luke 9:26), but also, redeemed men and women from the church age. John identifies these warrior/saints as he describes this future encounter between the returning Lamb of God and the nations that rage against him.

> *They will make war against the Lamb, but the Lamb will overcome them because he is Lord of lords and King of kings—with him will be his called, chosen and faithful followers.* –Revelation 17:14

> *The armies of heaven were following him, riding on white horses and dressed in fine linen, white and clean.* –Revelation 19:14

(Note: the "fine linen, white and clean" is an indication of a resurrected, redeemed person according to Revelation 19:8.)

> *May he strengthen your hearts so that you will be blameless and holy in the presence of our God and Father when our Lord Jesus comes with all his holy ones.* –First Thessalonians 3:13

The fact that this army that marches out with the Lord does indeed engage in battle can also be seen in this verse describing who the nations and their leaders will fight against on that day:

> *Then I saw the beast and the kings of the earth and their armies gathered together to make war against the rider on the horse and his army.* –Revelation 19:19

The Psalmist wrote:
> *Praise the Lord. Sing to the Lord a new song, his praise in the assembly of the saints. Let Israel rejoice in their Maker; let the people of Zion be glad in their king. . . . May the praise of God be in their mouths and a double-edged sword in their hands, to inflict vengeance on the nations and punishment on the peoples, to bind their kings with fetters, their nobles with shackles of iron, to carry out the sentence written against them. This is the glory of all his saints. Praise the Lord.* – Psalm 149:1, 2, 6-9

Paul questioned the Corinthians concerning their understanding of the future destiny and responsibility of the people of God when he wrote:

> *Do you not know that the saints will judge the world? And if you are to judge the world, are you not competent to judge trivial cases? Do you not know that we will judge angels?* –First Corinthians 6:2-3

An angel told Daniel:
> *The sovereignty, power and greatness of the kingdoms under the whole heaven will be handed over to the saints, the people of the Most High. His kingdom will be an everlasting kingdom, and all rulers will worship and obey him.* –Daniel 7:27

We can gain several additional insights into the Lord's military strategy, policy and weaponry from this battle. First we learn he has faithful insurgents placed within the enemy's territory on earth, that is, the people of Judah and Jerusalem. Second, we learn that the troops marching out of heaven with the Lord are well equipped. Most importantly, as citizens of the Lord's kingdom, they have been issued resurrection bodies.

Chapter 2 **The Ultimate Foreign Invasion**

> *Our citizenship is in heaven. And we eagerly await a Savior from there, the Lord Jesus Christ, who, by the power that enables him to bring everything under his control, will transform our lowly bodies so that they will be like his glorious body.* –Philippians 3:21

These resurrection bodies prove to be insurmountable in a battle against enemy troops equipped with bodies that can be "dissolved" as predicted by Zechariah:

> *This is the plague with which the Lord will strike all the nations that fought against Jerusalem: Their flesh will rot while they are still standing on their feet, their eyes will rot in their sockets, and their tongues will rot in their mouths.* –Zechariah 14:12

Also, these troops returning with the Lord seem to be individually equipped with a horse of equal status. These horses stand in stark contrast to the enemy horses, which are also easily liquefied.

> *. . . A similar plague will strike the horses and mules, the camels and donkeys, and all the animals in those camps.* –Zechariah 14:15

After this entrance campaign, the Lord will enter Jerusalem to be inaugurated as the King of Earth. Meanwhile military personal will be deployed throughout the earth for clean up operations and to root out any enemy supporters in other nations. This institutionalizing phase of kingdom policy is clearly laid out in the Lord's political platform as recorded throughout scripture.

Ezekiel captures Jesus' reentrance to Jerusalem to be seated on his throne in the temple. Ezekiel is standing in the temple courtyards on the Temple Mount in Jerusalem looking east toward the Mount of Olives when he receives a vision of this future day:

> Ezekiel: *Then the man brought me to the gate facing east, and I saw the glory of the God of Israel coming from the east (the Lord Jesus). His voice was like the roar of rushing waters, and the land was radiant with his glory . . . The glory of the Lord (Jesus) entered the temple through the gate facing east.*
>
> Lord: *Son of man, this is the place of my throne and the place for the soles of my feet. This is where I will live among the Israelites forever. The house of Israel will never again defile my holy name—neither they nor their kings.* –Ezekiel 43:1-7

Jesus himself spoke of the events that would follow after he is seated on the throne in the temple. He describes the events like this:

> *When the Son of Man comes in his glory, and all the angels with him, he will sit on his throne in heavenly glory. All the nations will be*

> gathered before him, and he will separate the people one from another as a shepherd separates the sheep from the goats. He will put the sheep on his right and the goats on his left. Then the King will say to those on his right, "Come, you who are blessed by my Father; take your inheritance, the kingdom prepared for you since the creation of the world" . . . Then he will say to those on his left, "Depart from me, you who are cursed, into the eternal fire prepared for the devil and his angels." –Matthew 25:31-34, 41

The criterion on which the Lord bases his decision is how these individual people treated the Jews (or "these brothers of mine" as seen in Matthew 25:40; Joel 3:2) during the events leading up to his return. This teaching of Jesus is found in his discourse on End Times events in Matthew 24 and 25. Jesus' presentation of the sheep and goat judgment is not as much a parable that needs to be unraveled as it is a prophecy of actual events that will take place when he returns. It should be read and understood this way. The use of the imagery of the sheep and goats is taken from Ezekiel's prophecy concerning the same events (Ezekiel 34:17-31).

It is clear that all the nations' military leaders stood against Jesus and the Jewish people, but within each of those nations there are going to be believers who responded with support for the Lord and his chosen people in the last days.

Search and seize missions will be conducted throughout the earth to gather people for the sheep and goat judgment described in Matthew 25:31. The people of the nations will respond to the king's return, and detachments of troops will be sent out just like Isaiah describes:

> Men will flee to caves in the rocks and to holes in the ground from dread of the Lord and the splendor of his majesty, when he rises to shake the earth. In that day men will throw away to the rodents and bats their idols of silver and idols of gold, which they made to worship. They will flee to caverns in the rocks and to the overhanging crags from dread of the Lord and the splendor of his majesty, when he rises to shake the earth. –Isaiah 2:19-21

> In those days and at that time, when I restore the fortunes of Judah and Jerusalem, I will gather all nations and bring them down to the Valley of Jehoshaphat ("the Lord judges"). There I will enter into judgment against them concerning my inheritance, my people Israel. –Joel 3:1, 2

Zechariah says:

> Survivors from all the nations that have attacked Jerusalem will go up year after year to worship the King, the Lord Almighty, and to celebrate the Feast of Tabernacles. –Zechariah 14:16

Chapter 2 The Ultimate Foreign Invasion

Isaiah says:

> In that day the Branch of the Lord will be beautiful and glorious, and the fruit of the land will be the pride and glory of the survivors in Israel. Those who are left in Zion, who remain in Jerusalem, will be called holy, all who are recorded among the living in Jerusalem.
> –Isaiah 4:2-3

Isaiah also predicts the government and rule of the Lord and King in an earthly kingdom:

> For to us a child is born, to us a son is given, and the government will be on his shoulders. And he will be called Wonderful Counselor, Mighty God, Everlasting Father, Prince or Peace. Of the increase of his government and peace there will be no end. He will reign on David's throne and over his kingdom, establishing and upholding it with justice and righteousness from that time on and forever.
> –Isaiah 9:6-7

There is abundant testimony in both the Old and New Testaments concerning the Lord's coming kingdom. The nations have been warned in scripture. Part of our testimony to the people of the world and to the nations of the world is to proclaim this truth: The Lord is coming back from heaven to overthrow his enemies and set up a world-dominating empire. The Lord will be king over the whole earth. This good news of the kingdom will be proclaimed.

Today the church should proclaim the good news of salvation through faith in Jesus Christ so the nations can hear about Jesus' coming kingdom just like they did from David as we read in Psalms 2. The church must share the gospel before the end comes.

> This gospel of the kingdom will be preached in the whole world as a testimony to all nations, and then the end will come. –Matthew 24:14

> At that time the sign of the Son of Man will appear in the sky, and all the nations of the earth will mourn. They will see the Son of Man coming on the clouds of the sky, with power and great glory. –Matthew 24:30

> God is just: He will pay back trouble to those who trouble you and give relief to you who are troubled, and to us as well. This will happen when the Lord Jesus is revealed from heaven in blazing fire with his powerful angels. He will punish those who do not know God and do not obey the gospel of our Lord Jesus. They will be punished with everlasting destruction and shut out from the presence of the Lord and from the majesty of his power on the day he comes to be glorified in his holy people and to be marveled at among all those who have believed.
> –II Thessalonians 1:7-8

Then the lawless one will be revealed, whom the Lord Jesus will overthrow with the breath of his mouth and destroy by the splendor of his coming. –II Thessalonians 2:8

He will be great and will be called the Son of the Most High. The Lord God will give him the throne of his father David, and he will reign over the house of Jacob forever; his kingdom will never end. –Luke 1:32

The days are coming when I will raise up to David a righteous Branch, a King who will reign wisely and do what is just and right in the land. In his days Judah will be saved and Israel will live in safety. This is the name by which he will be called: The Lord Our Righteousness.
–Jeremiah 23:5-6

With your blood you purchased men for God from every tribe and language and people and nation. You have made them to be a kingdom and priests to serve our God, and they will reign on the earth. –Revelation 5:10

> *Clap your hands, all you nations;*
> *shout to God with cries of joy.*
> *How awesome is the Lord Most High,*
> *the great King over all the earth!*
> *He subdued nations under us,*
> *peoples under our feet.*
> *He chose our inheritance for us,*
> *the pride of Jacob, whom he loved*
>   *Selah*
>
> *God has ascended amid shouts of joy,*
> *the Lord amid the sounding of trumpets.*
> *Sing praises to God, sing praises;*
> *sing praises to our King, sing praises.*
>
> *For God is the King of all the earth;*
> *sing to him a psalm of praise.*
> *God reigns over the nations;*
> *God is seated on his holy throne.*
> *The nobles of the nations assemble*
> *as the people of the God of Abraham,*
> *for the kings of the earth belong to God;*
> *he is greatly exalted.* –Psalm 47

Chapter Three
The Decline of Authority

The future establishment of the Lord's kingdom and the implementation of his political agenda on earth were revealed to Nebuchadnezzar in the second year of his reign around 604 or 603 BC. This vision is recorded in Daniel 2. Nebuchadnezzar not only ruled a nation, he ruled many nations that he had gathered into what was known as the Babylonian empire. Daniel describes a dream that Nebuchadnezzar had like this:

> As you were lying there, O king, your mind turned to things to come, and the revealer of mysteries showed you what is going to happen . . . You looked, O king, and there before you stood a large statue—an enormous dazzling statue, awesome in appearance. The head of the statue was made of pure gold, its chest and arms of silver, its belly and thighs of bronze, its legs of iron, its feet partly of iron and partly of baked clay. While you were watching, a rock was cut out, but not by human hands. It struck the stature on its feet of iron and clay and smashed them. Then the iron, the clay, the bronze, the silver and the gold were broken to pieces at the same time and became like chaff on a threshing floor in the summer. The wind swept them away without leaving a trace. But the rock that struck the statue became a huge mountain and filled the whole earth. –Daniel 2:29-35

The statue that Nebuchadnezzar saw consisted of a head of gold, a chest of silver, a waist of bronze, two legs of iron and feet of iron mixed with clay. This statue was attacked, destroyed and completely removed by a rock that struck the statue at its weakest point, the feet. Then, in the place the statue had stood, the rock became a mountain that covered the earth.

Nebuchadnezzar was not sure what the dream meant, but he had a feeling it was a bad omen for him. Was he the statue? Was Egypt the rock? Were his court magicians plotting to overthrow him? He needed to figure out what the rock and the statue represented. Daniel then gave Nebuchadnezzar the interpretation.

> You, O king, are the king of kings. The God of heaven has given you dominion and power and might and glory; in your hands he has placed mankind and the beasts of the field and the birds of the air. Wherever they live, he has made you ruler over them all. You are that head of gold. –Daniel 2:36-38

The golden head of the statue represented Nebuchadnezzar and his empire. God had given Nebuchadnezzar total control of the earth. That did not mean it was easy, nor did that mean everyone submitted to him. We know from the Bible and other historical documents that the Middle East (Judah, Moab, Ammon, Phoenicia, etc.) was constantly revolting against Nebuchadnezzar. Egypt even appeared to strike a deathblow to his military within a few months of this dream

(601 BC). Yet Nebuchadnezzar had been given dominion by God and would ultimately succeed. He had ultimate rule. His word was law. He and his empire are described as "gold." Not only is gold the most valuable of the materials in the statue, gold is also the densest and softest (most workable, pliable, useful) of all the materials that make up the statue.

Daniel continues to explain the dream to Nebuchadnezzar:
> *After you, another kingdom will rise, inferior to yours. Next, a third kingdom, one of bronze, will rule over the whole earth. Finally there will be a fourth kingdom, strong as iron—for iron breaks and smashes everything— and as iron breaks things to pieces, so it will crush and break all the others. Just as you saw that the feet and toes were partly of baked clay and partly of iron, so this will be a divided kingdom; yet it will have some of the strength of iron in it, even as you saw iron mixed with clay. As the toes were partly iron and partly clay, so this kingdom will be partly strong and partly brittle. And just as you saw the iron mixed with baked clay, so the people will be a mixture and will not remain united, any more than iron mixes with clay.* –Daniel 2:39-43

A statement worthy of note in Daniel's explanation of the dream is "another kingdom will rise, inferior to yours." The kingdoms that followed Babylon were Persia (the chest of silver), Greece (the waist of bronze) and Rome (the legs of iron). Each one of these empires covered more territory and endured more years than Babylon. Babylon's empire lasted from 627-539 BC (88 years) while Persia's empire extended from 539 to 331 BC (208 years), and Greece's empire from 331 to 31 BC (300 years), and Rome's from 31 BC to 476 AD (507 years) in the West and 31 BC to 1453 AD (1,484 years) in the East.

Persia, Greece and Rome had superior sized territory and a longer length of rule. So how were they inferior? The authority of the king diminished as each empire gave way to the next. Nebuchadnezzar established his law with a simple command. He could order the execution of all the wise men in the land (as seen in Daniel 2:12) and then change his mind and renounce the command (Daniel 2:46-49). Nebuchadnezzar had absolute authority. That is not to say he was always right or just; but he was always absolute.

Note that when Persia emerged, the ruler could sign a law, but once that law went into effect the Persian ruler could not change it. Here are a couple of examples: First, consider Daniel 6 when Darius the Persian was manipulated into signing a law that would send anyone who prayed to any other god into the lion's den. When Darius found out Daniel would be the one fed to the lions, Darius could not change the law even though he wanted to:

> *The decree stands—in accordance with the laws of the Medes and Persians, which cannot be repealed.* –Daniel 6:12; 6:8

Chapter 3 **The Decline of Authority**

The same was true of Xerxes in the book of Esther. After decrees *"were written in the name of King Xerxes himself and sealed with his own ring…to destroy, kill and annihilate all the Jews, young and old, women and little children, on a single day, the thirteenth day of the twelfth month, the month of Adar, and to plunder their goods…"* (Esther 3:13) this decree could not be changed. Even when Xerxes found out Esther, his queen, was Jewish and Haman was an evil man, the law could not be changed. So the king had Mordecai write a new edict that granted the Jews in every city the right to assemble and protect themselves; to destroy, kill and annihilate any armed force of any nationality or province that might attack them and their women and children; and to plunder the property of their enemies (Esther 8:11-12).

Overthrowing the Persian rulers were the Greeks. The Greeks are known as the founders of democracy. Their kings did not make the laws, their people did. And following the Greek empire came the mighty Roman Empire. The Roman standard marched across the world engraved with the letters SPQR—"The Senate and People of Rome" (Latin: Senatus Populusque Romanus). As a republic, Rome's authority came from the people and not a king or emperor. This is the basis for our modern democratic ideas. In the United States, we too believe that power rests with the people and not in one man.

As shown in Nebuchadnezzar's statue, the authority of an absolute monarch in Babylon devolved into the will of the people in the modern world. The statue stands on a base of baked, brittle clay mixed with iron. The final days of the rule of the empires are represented by brittle clay mixed with iron. The brittle feet and toes symbolize a time when a wide range of people will come together to unite their values, views, opinions and political platforms in an attempt to organize and rule the earth. What does the Lord think of this? He calls the absolute rule of Nebuchadnezzar gold and the rule of these people worthless.

I think it is worth noting here that when the Lord addresses the final age of church history, which is represented by the Laodicean church in Asia around 96 AD, he has nothing positive to say (Revelation 3:14-22). The name "Laodicea" itself comes from two words: "laos" meaning "people" and "dike" meaning "decision." The word "Laodicea" then translates to "people ruled."

The scriptures indicate that the Lord's political platform is much closer to Nebuchadnezzar's than a people-ruled democracy. Indeed, a form of democracy has served the United States well, but it was a democracy based on Christian principles and a Biblical worldview. It was developed with the understanding that we lived under the ultimate rule of the Lord and King, Jesus Christ. As western democracy radically departs from these core beliefs, we will continue to see the brittle clay weaken human society.

The Political Platform of the Lord and King

Besides the inevitable collapse of modern society into chaos, the greatest disaster for nations in the future will be the climatic events in Daniel's dream:

> *Just as you saw the iron mixed with baked clay, so the people will be a mixture and will not remain united, any more than iron mixes with clay. In the time of those kings, the God of heaven will set up a kingdom that will never be destroyed, nor will it be left to another people. It will crush all those kingdoms and bring them to an end, but it will itself endure forever. This is the meaning of the vision of the rock cut out of a mountain, but not by human hands—a rock that broke the iron, the bronze, the clay, the silver and the gold to pieces.* –Daniel 2:43-45

The rock cut out of the mountain that strikes the brittle clay is the invasion of the Lord and King, Jesus Christ. (Remember the Mount of Olives episode?) He will establish a kingdom in the place of the Babylonian, Persian, Grecian and Roman empires—a kingdom that will reign over the whole world. Understand this: The rapture (if you believe in it) is not an evacuation plan; it is a declaration of war on the kingdoms of this world by the kingdom of God. Likewise, the second coming is not a spiritual nullification of the present physical reality; it is a full-scale invasion of planet earth and a universal takeover of this world's kingdoms.

We need to stop making this more complicated than it is. The Lord and King, Jesus Christ, is coming back to take over. We must not let it become an exercise in a spiritual dismissal of reality. It is as clear as Job claimed it to be:

> *I know that my Redeemer lives, and that in the end he will stand upon the earth. And after my skin has been destroyed, yet in my flesh I will see God; I myself will see him with my own eyes—I, and not another. How my heart yearns within me!* –Job 19:25-27

Well said, Job!

Daniel then ends his interpretation of the dream by saying:

> *The great God has shown the king what will take place in the future. The dream is true and the interpretation is trustworthy.* –Daniel 2:45

The Lord and King's political platform does not include the modern concept of democracy, or "Laodicea." Though citizens of the Lord's kingdom will have freedom, they will not be expressing themselves politically by campaigning, polling or voting. Eventually there will be people born and raised in the Lord's kingdom that will disagree with his administration. Some will grow to despise the King, but no one will burn the kingdom's flag more than once and there will be no freedom of speech allowed in the way we understand it. There will be no talk radio, no opinion pages in the newspaper, no Internet blog posts that could undermine the Lord's methods or question the King's integrity.

Chapter 3 The Decline of Authority

Let us keep some verses in mind:
> *You will rule them with an iron scepter; you will dash them to pieces like pottery.* –Psalm 2:9

> *The Lord will be king over the whole earth. On that day there will be one Lord, and his name the only name.* –Zechariah 14:9

> *The Lord alone will be exalted in that day.* –Isaiah 2:11

> *The Lord alone will be exalted in that day, and the idols will totally disappear.* –Isaiah 2:17, 18

> *The Lord reigns, let the nations tremble. He sits enthroned between the cherubim, let the earth shake. Great is the Lord in Zion; he is exalted over all the nations.* –Psalm 99:1-2

> *If any of the peoples of the earth do not go up to Jerusalem to worship the King, the Lord Almighty, they will have no rain. If the Egyptian people do not go up and take part, they will have no rain. The Lord will bring on them the plague he inflicts on the nations that do not go up to celebrate the Feast of Tabernacles.* This will be the punishment of Egypt and the punishment of all the nations that do not go up to celebrate the Feast of Tabernacles.** –Zechariah 14:17-19

(*The Feast of Tabernacles is a public holiday that celebrates the Lord dwelling among man. It is a seven-day feast during harvest. King Solomon dedicated the Temple in Jerusalem during this holiday and the Lord's presence came into the Temple at that time. The Feast of Tabernacles is a celebration of the arrival of the Lord and King and a time for rejoicing concerning the abundance and peace his presence has brought to the earth.)

> *Then the sovereignty, power and greatness of the kingdoms under the whole heaven will be handed over to the saints, the people of the Most High. His kingdom will be an everlasting kingdom, and all rulers will worship and obey him.* –Daniel 7:27

> *All kings will bow down to him and all nations will serve him.* –Psalm 72:11

> *Just and true are your ways, King of the ages.*
> *Who will not fear you, O Lord, and bring glory to your name?*
> *For you alone are holy, All nations will come and worship before you for your righteous acts have been revealed.* –Revelation 15:3-4
> *Then you will know that I, the Lord your God, dwell in Zion, my holy hill. Jerusalem will be holy; never again will foreigners invade her . . .*
> *The Lord dwells in Zion!* –Joel 3:17, 21

The Political Platform of the Lord and King

The name of the city from that time on will be: THE LORD IS THERE.
–Ezekiel 48:35

> *Arise, shine, for your light has come,*
> *and the glory of the Lord rises upon you.*
> *See, darkness covers the earth*
> *and thick darkness is over the peoples,*
> *but the Lord rises upon you*
> *and his glory appears over you.*
> *Nations will come to your light,*
> *and kings to the brightness of your dawn.*
> *–Isaiah 60:1-3*

Chapter Four
The Policies of the Lord's Administration

We have seen the Lord as the invader of the earth. We have seen him as the ruthless conquering warrior. He has been revealed as the judge and jury of the nations he has conquered. It is clear his rule will have complete dominion over the earth and over all the national governments that he brings under the umbrella of his authority. Jesus is the Lord and King on earth. There is no other name. There is no other political party. Any opposition will be crushed like pottery being smashed on the ground.

Once his authority has been established and his position as world ruler has been secured, what will his governmental policies be? How will his administration handle all the issues he will inherit? The answers to these questions are found in the writings of prophets like Isaiah, Ezekiel, Micah and others.

Here, based on the writings of those prophets, is the Lord and King's political platform concerning 37 key issues:

1. Affirmative Action - Affirmative action takes race, religion, sex or national origin into consideration to increase the representation of minorities in areas where they have previously been excluded.

It appears that individuals within the nations are evaluated on their individual merits, as seen at the sheep and goat judgment, so the concept of Affirmative Action really has no place in how the King evaluates the people.

> *All the nations will be gathered before him, and he will separate the people one from another.* –Matthew 25:31

Also, when it comes to positions of service in the temple located in the center of the capital city of Jerusalem—only men from the family of Zadok are allowed to serve as priests. There are no women priests. There are no priests from any people group other than the Jews, and there are no priests from any other tribe of Israel except the tribe of Levi. Even Levites who are not from the family of Aaron cannot serve as priests.

> *These are the sons of Zadok, who are the only Levites who may draw near to the Lord to minister before him.* –Ezekiel 40:46 (also 43:19; 44:15)

Thus, affirmative action, as we understand it today, has no place in the kingdom of the Lord and King. There will be very strict "discrimination" based on race and sex in certain areas. But there is no discrimination at all in terms of merit or judgment.

2. Agriculture – Agricultural production will increase under the Lord's reign because he will control not only the weather and the topography, but also the sun and the moon. The Lord will increase production by intensifying the process of photosynthesis. After the Lord's return, he will also increase the flow of water.

> *He will also send you rain for the seed you sow in the ground, and the food that comes from the land will be rich and plentiful. In that day your cattle will graze in broad meadows. The oxen and donkeys that work the soil will eat fodder and mash, spread out with fork and shovel. In the day of great slaughter, when the towers fall, streams of water will flow on every high mountain and every lofty hill. The moon will shine like the sun, and the sunlight will be seven times brighter, like the light of seven full days.* –Isaiah 30:23-26

The Lord will control the agricultural production across the globe and will demand a portion of the produce from each nation be presented to him during the Feast of Tabernacles held annually in Jerusalem.

> *If any of the people of the earth do not go up to Jerusalem to worship the King, the Lord Almighty, they will have no rain . . . The Lord will bring on them the plague he inflicts on the nations that do not go up to celebrate the Feast of Tabernacles.* –Zechariah 14:18

3. Animal Rights - Because of the increase in fresh water on earth, there will be a much larger fish population. But the fish will be caught and used for food.

> *"There will be large numbers of fish, because this water flows there and makes the salt water fresh; so where the river flows everything will live. Fishermen will stand along the shore; from En Gedi to En Eglaim there will be places for spreading nets.* –Ezekiel 47:9, 10

Temple services will resume in Jerusalem and the sacrifice of animals will be extensive. Sacrificing animals will be viewed as a legal and acceptable way to worship the Lord and King and to commemorate his personal death and sacrifice on the cross. This practice is detailed in several places in Ezekiel 40-48.

> *You are to take the bull for the sin offering and burn it in the designated part of the temple area outside the sanctuary.* –Ezekiel 43:21

> *On the day of the New Moon he is to offer a young bull, six lambs and a ram, all without defect.* –Ezekiel 46:6

> *Also one sheep is to be taken from every flock of two hundred from the well-watered pastures of Israel. These will be used for the grain offerings, burnt offerings and fellowship offerings to make atonement for the people, declares the Sovereign Lord.* –Ezekiel 45:15

30   Chapter 4 **The Policies of the Lord's Administration**

The Lord will also change the natural state of animals, or it could be said, restore the original state of animals, so it will be in line with his plans and purposes:

> *The wolf will live with the lamb, the leopard will lie down with the goat, the calf and the lion and the yearling together; and a little child will lead them. The cow will feed with the bear, their young will lie down together, and the lion will eat straw like the ox. The infant will play near the hole of the cobra, and the young child put his hand into the viper's next. They will neither harm nor destroy on all my holy mountain.* –Isaiah 11:6-9

4. Budget - in this age of prosperity and production, the government's budget is never mentioned. It would appear from other references that records are kept and money is well managed, but the size of the budget is not indicated. It would likely be extravagant, especially if Solomon's budget that we read about in I Kings is considered to be a shadow or type.

> *The people of Judah and Israel were as numerous as the sand on the seashore; they ate, they drank and they were happy. And Solomon ruled over all the kingdoms from the River to the land of the Philistines, as far as the border of Egypt. These countries brought tribute and were Solomon's subjects all his life. Solomon's daily provisions were thirty cors (185 bushels) of fine flour and sixty cors (375 bushels) of meal, ten head of stall-fed cattle, twenty of pasture-fed cattle and a hundred sheep and goats, as well as deer, gazelles, roebucks and choice fowl. For he ruled over all the kingdoms west of the River, from Tiphsah to Gaza, and had peace on all sides. During Solomon's lifetime Judah and Israel, from Dan to Beersheba, lived in safety, each man under his own vine and fig tree. Solomon had four thousand stalls for chariot horses, and twelve thousand horses. The district officers, each in his month, supplied provisions for King Solomon and all who came to the king's table. They saw to it that nothing was lacking. They also brought to the proper place their quotas of barley and straw for the chariot horses and the other horses."* –I Kings 4:20-28

5. Censorship - The kingdom's political policy concerning censorship is not explicitly stated, but the suppression of speech or destruction of materials designed to communicate objectionable, harmful, immoral or blasphemous messages is highly likely. Consider this verse:

> *You will rule them with an iron scepter.* –Psalm 2:9

It is worth noting though that at the end of a thousand year period, the nations that have been ruled with an iron scepter are allowed to be deceived. They will then march in rebellion on Jerusalem against the throne of the Lord and King. It is hard to imagine this kind of rebellion and organization occurring without some form of freedom of press and speech.

> When the thousand years are over, Satan will be released from his prison and will go out to deceive the nations in the four corners of the earth—Gog and Magog—to gather them for battle. In number they are like the sand of the seashore. They march across the breadth of the earth and surround the camp of God's people, the city he loves. – Revelation 20:7-10

6. The Separation of Church and State - In the kingdom of the Lord and King there will be no separation of government from religion. The very fact that the Lord who is worshipped and the King who rules is the same person makes it impossible to separate the two. Religion is the source of the state. The state is an expression of the religion. The religion is truth and reality and the state is prosperous and at peace.

> The prince himself is the only one who may sit inside the gateway to eat in the presence of the Lord. He is to enter by way of the portico of the gateway and go out the same way. –Ezekiel 44:3-4

The throne of the king (the state) sits inside the temple (the church).

> Son of man, this is the place of my throne and the place for the soles of my feet. This is where I will live among the Israelites forever. –Ezekiel 43:6

All the people will worship the Lord and King on the Sabbath Day.

> On the Sabbaths and New Moons the people of the land are to worship in the presence of the Lord at the entrance to that gateway. –Ezekiel 46:3

The King will establish religious holidays and rituals.

> Then he said to me, "Son of man, this is what the Sovereign Lord says: These will be the regulations for sacrificing burnt offerings and sprinkling blood upon the altar when it is built" ... –Ezekiel 43:18, 22, 25, 27

7. Crime - There will be secure locations where the public can travel and live without any fear of crime.

> And a highway will be there; it will be called the Way of Holiness. The unclean will not journey on it; it will be for those who walk in that Way; wicked fools will not go about on it. No lion will be there, nor will any ferocious beast get up on it; they will not be found there. –Isaiah 35:8, 9

There will be no harm or destruction in the capital city of Jerusalem—a city that will be visited by people from every nation on a regular basis.

Chapter 4 The Policies of the Lord's Administration

> *"They will neither harm nor destroy on all my holy mountain", says the Lord.* –Isaiah 65:25

8. Death Penalty – Individuals who rebel against the Lord and King during his reign on earth may face capital punishment. Apparently, longevity will be one of the many social benefits resulting from the implementation of the Lord's political policies.

> *He who fails to reach a hundred will be considered accursed.*
> –Isaiah 65:20

But rebels will still be executed under the iron scepter rule of the King. The death penalty will be used by this administration.

> *"All mankind will come and bow down before me," says the Lord. "And they will go out and look upon the dead bodies of those who rebelled against me; their worm will not die, nor will their fire be quenched, and they will be loathsome to all mankind."* –Isaiah 66:23-24

There will be death in the Lord's kingdom because the final enemy to be conquered is death itself, and that won't happen until the end of the one thousand year reign when Jesus will hand the kingdom over to God the Father and exchange it for a new heaven and earth (1 Corinthians 15:24-28).

In Ezekiel 40-48 where the new temple for the Lord's reign on earth is discussed, the regulations for priests are also explained:

> *A priest must not defile himself by going near a dead person; however, if the dead person was his father or mother, son or daughter, brother or unmarried sister, then he may defile himself. After he is cleansed, he must wait seven days.* –Ezekiel 44:25

9. Drugs – There will be a kind of medication used in the kingdom.

> *Fruit trees of all kinds will grow on both banks of the river. Their leaves will not wither, nor will their fruit fail. Every month they will bear, because the water from the sanctuary flows to them. Their fruit will serve for food and their leaves for healing.* –Ezekiel 47:12

The Lord's view of drugs for mystical, magical or mind-altering experiences has always been very negative. The Lord has never shown any support for the use of drugs in immoral ways during previous administrations (New Testament, Old Testament or even in a future eternal state). It would be assumed that the political platform of the Lord during his administration on earth would maintain a similar policy.

New Testament: *The acts of the sinful nature are obvious . . . idolatry and witchcraft.* (Galatians 5:19, 20—Greek: "pharmakeia" which is where our English word "pharmacy" comes from. "Pharmakeia" referred to sorcery or enchantment along with the use of medicine, drugs and spells.)

> Old Testament: *Let no one be found among you who sacrifices his son or daughter in the fire, who practices divination or sorcery, interprets omens, engages in witchcraft, or casts spells, or who is a medium or spiritist or who consults the dead. Anyone who does these things is detestable to the Lord, and because of these detestable practices the Lord your God will drive out those nations before you.* –Deuteronomy 18:10-14

> Eternal State: *But the cowardly, the unbelieving, the vile, the murderers, the sexually immoral, those who practice magic arts, the idolaters and all liars—their place will be in the fiery lake of burning sulfur.* –Revelation 21:8

10. Disarmament, Military, Gun Control, War - Under the Lord's rule, nations will disarm themselves, either willingly or by force. Regardless, all the militaries of all nations will be disarmed. Nations will not be able, nor will they be allowed, to take up arms against each other in military conflicts. There will be no war between nations. Any disputes will be directed to the Lord and King in Jerusalem for resolution.

> *He will judge between the nations and will settle disputes for many peoples. They will beat their swords into plowshares and their spears into pruning hooks. Nation will not take up sword against nation, nor will they train for war anymore.* –Isaiah 2:4

Notice, what this does not say. It does not say the Lord will lay down his weapons or cease to be prepared for war. The Lord and King who is ruling with an iron scepter and who has crushed all the opposition never disarms. The King's political slogan concerning international weapons is: "None for you, all for us!"

> *Rise and thresh, O Daughter of Zion, for I will give you horns of iron; I will give you hoofs of bronze and you will break to pieces many nations.* –Micah 4:13

> *Your troops will be willing on your day of battle.* –Psalm 110:3

The King will have a powerful, well-equipped military that is invincible. The strength of his military is found in its citizen soldiers (Rev. 19:14) and in its angelic forces whose superiority is unmatched. Not to mention the leader of the military is the greatest warrior of all time—the Lord himself. Because of this there will be no need for conquered nations to maintain their own futile militaries, nor will they be allowed to.

Chapter 4 The Policies of the Lord's Administration

11. Economy, National Debt - Everything the Lord does will benefit his kingdom's economy. These things include: the way he governs, the way he empowers the weak, the information he communicates to his people, the changes he makes in the environment, the alterations he makes to the climate, the standard of righteousness lived out by the citizens of his kingdom, and much more. Trade from the south, east and even the west will come into Jerusalem. All these things will contribute to an economy that will be by far the greatest the earth has ever seen.

> *Then you will look and be radiant, your heart will throb and swell with joy; the wealth on the seas will be brought to you, to you the riches of the nations will come. Herds of camels will cover your land, young camels of Midian and Ephah. And all from Sheba will come, bearing gold and incense and proclaiming the praise of the Lord. All Kedar's flocks will be gathered to you, the rams of Nebaioth will serve you; they will be accepted as offerings on my altar, and I will adorn my glorious temple. Who are these that fly along like clouds, like doves to their nests? Surely the islands look to me; in the lead are the ships of Tarshish, bringing your sons from afar, with their silver and gold, the honor of the Lord your God, the Holy One of Israel, for he has endowed you with splendor.* –Isaiah 60;4-9

A few things to be noted here concerning the Lord's economy are:
    1) the importance of gold being traded as a commodity
    2) the importance of international trade
    3) the practice of free trade between countries
    4) the freedom of business corporations to compete

There will be no debt in the nations that honor the Lord. Gold and silver will be the standard of exchange. International trade will be abundant and will spread prosperity throughout the Lord's reign.

> *All from Sheba will come, bearing gold and incense and proclaiming the praise of the Lord.* –Isaiah 60:6

> *Surely the islands look to me; in the lead are the ships of Tarshish, bringing your sons from afar, with their silver and gold, to the honor of the Lord your God, the Holy One of Israel, for he has endowed you with splendor.* –Isaiah 60:9

12. Education - The Lord's knowledge will be sought by every nation. Educators and researchers will come to Jerusalem to question, interview and explore the Lord's ideas and thoughts. The Lord will provide information for business, agriculture, scientific research, social issues and all other areas of academia. Nations will send representatives to Jerusalem to secure an audience with the Lord and gain insight into their problems and questions.

> *Many peoples will come and say, "Come, let us go up to the mountain of the Lord, to the house of the God of Jacob. He will teach us his ways, so that we may walk in his paths."* –Isaiah 2:3; Micah 4:2

The earth will be greatly influenced by the Lord's educational philosophy and the content of his curriculum. The earth will be filled with his teachings and with a knowledge of his truth. The result will be a golden age for earth when it comes to social development, economic growth and prosperity, research and development and international trade and cooperation.

> *They will neither harm nor destroy on all my holy mountain, for the earth will be full of the knowledge of the Lord as the waters cover the sea.* –Isaiah 11:9

Teachers from the King's court in Jerusalem will be sent into all the earth to teach the nations.

> *I will send some of those who survive to the nations—to Tarshish, to the Libyans and Lydians (famous as archers), to Tubal and Greece, and to the distant islands that have not heard of my fame or seen my glory.* – Isaiah 66:19

The priests who are descendants of Zadok and who served the Lord faithfully when the Israelites went astray will teach the people and settle any disputes concerning education and the law.

> *The priests, who are Levites and descendants of Zadok and who faithfully carried out the duties of my sanctuary when the Israelites went astray from me ...are to teach my people the difference between the holy and the common and show them how to distinguish between the unclean and the clean. In any dispute, the priests are to serve as judges and decide it according to my ordinances.* –Ezekiel 44:15, 23, 24

13. Environment - The environment will be arranged and used for the administration's political purposes and plans. But understand the Lord does not destroy the earth; he simply has dominion over it. This was what Adam was originally supposed to do. The Lord will alter and use the earth, but he won't harm it in any way. In fact, part of his judgment will be against those who did not manage the earth but instead destroyed it.

> *The nations were angry and your wrath has come. The time has come ...for destroying those who destroy the earth.* –Revelation 11:18

The landscape around the capital city of Jerusalem will be physically altered in order to raise Jerusalem up on a mountain.

> *In the last days the mountain of the Lord's temple will be established as chief among the mountains; it will be raised above the hills, and all nations will stream to it.* –Isaiah 2:2

36   Chapter 4   The Policies of the Lord's Administration

Ezekiel is taken in a vision to Jerusalem to see what it is like after the events of Zechariah 14 and the Lord's return have occurred. In this future vision, the city is high on a mountain with homes and buildings on the southern slope of the mountain.

> *In visions of God he took me to the land of Israel and set me on a very high mountain on whose south side were some buildings that looked like a city.* –Ezekiel 40:2 (also 43:12)

One of the plans of this new administration is to turn Jerusalem into a seaport. Reminiscent of the original Garden in Eden, a waterway will be formed to connect the capital city of Jerusalem to the Mediterranean Sea and the Indian Ocean by way of the Dead Sea through the Red Sea. The water source will originate on the Temple Mount and it will flow out of the temple toward the east.

The water will flow from the temple and progressively get deeper the further away it gets from the Temple Mount. The water will be ankle deep for the first quarter of a mile from the temple. It will be knee deep at the half-mile mark. By the time the water reaches three-quarters of a mile from the temple, it will be waist deep. At the mile mark, a person will have to swim—although it will be impossible to swim across this river. (Ezekiel 47:3-5). This water will fill up the Jordan Valley (Ezekiel 47:8) and the Dead Sea. It will then continue to flow south and empty into the Gulf of Aqaba in the Red Sea, which connects to the Indian Ocean.

> *The man brought me back to the entrance of the temple, and I saw water coming out from under the threshold of the temple toward the east. The water was coming down from under the south side of the temple, south of the altar ...He said to me, "This water flows toward the eastern region and goes down into the Arabah (Jordan Valley), where it enters the Sea (Dead Sea). When it empties into the Sea, the water there becomes fresh. Swarms of living creatures will live wherever the river flows. There will be large numbers of fish, because this water flows there and makes the salt water fresh; so where the river flows everything will live . . . But the swamps and marshes will not become fresh; they will be left for salt. Fruit trees of all kinds will grow on both banks of the river.* –Ezekiel 47:1-12

The Lord's environmental policy will not only accommodate his kingdom's desires and needs, but will also be extremely environmentally friendly. His policy is based on the philosophy of change. Change the land, change the mountains and redirect the rivers to improve cities, businesses, agriculture and jobs! "Change Our Land; Improve Our Lives!"

Notice the extra care taken for the preservation of the salt swamps. This is, most likely, for business and production reasons. The addition of commercial fishing in the Dead Sea will be a huge economic boost. The Lord's environmental adjustments cause the fruit trees to produce twelve crops a year instead of only one. This is a 1200% improvement on production. That should also boost an already robust economy. In addition to the production of fruit, the leaves of these trees will help support the kingdom's health care plan because they contain medicinal properties discovered by the kingdom's medical research team.

The topography change that elevates Jerusalem and converts it into a seaport is supported in other scriptures:

> *In that day the mountains will drip new wine, and the hills will flow with milk; all the ravines of Judah will run with water. A fountain will flow out of the Lord's house and will water the valley of acacias.* –Joel 3:18

> *In the last days the mountain of the Lord's temple will be established as chief among the mountains; it will be raised above the hills.* –Isaiah 2:2

> *In visions of God he took me to the land of Israel and set me on a very high mountain on whose south side were some buildings that looked like a city . . . I saw a wall completely surrounding the temple area . . .* –Ezekiel 40:2

> *On that day living water will flow out from Jerusalem, half to the eastern sea (Dead Sea) and half to the western sea (Mediterranean Sea), in summer and in winter.* –Zechariah 14:8

14. Equal Opportunities, Equal Rights - The government officials will not oppress the people through overbearing taxation, forced labor, inconsistent scales or confiscation of property.

> *Every man will sit under his own vine and under his own fig tree, and no one will make them afraid.* –Micah 4:4

> *My princes will no longer oppress my people but will allow the house of Israel to possess the land according to their tribes. This is what the Sovereign Lord says, "You have gone far enough, O princes of Israel! Give up your violence and oppression and do what is just and right. Stop dispossessing my people," declares the Sovereign Lord. "You are to use accurate scales.* –Ezekiel 45:8-10

The land of Israel will be equally divided among the tribes.

> *You are to divide it equally among them. Because I swore with uplifted hand to give it to your forefathers, this land will become your inheritance.* –Ezekiel 47:14

Chapter 4 The Policies of the Lord's Administration

Aliens are also given land.

> *You are to allot it as an inheritance for yourselves and for the aliens who have settled among you and who have children. You are to consider them as native-born Israelites; along with you they are to be allotted an inheritance among the tribes of Israel.* –Ezekiel 47:22

But, not everyone can be a priest and not everyone can enter the temple sanctuary.

> *No foreigner uncircumcised in heart and flesh is to enter my sanctuary.*
> –Ezekiel 44:9

15. Euthanasia - In the Lord and King's administration elderly people will not be overlooked or eliminated. Instead they will be well cared for and equipped with what they need to live, prosper and enjoy kingdom society.

> *Once again men and women of ripe old age will sit in the streets of Jerusalem, each with cane in hand because of his age.* –Zechariah 8:4

16. Families and Children – The kingdom shows favor to families, and children will be a priority.

> *The city streets will be filled with boys and girls playing there.*
> –Zechariah 8:5

Families build homes and live together. They will lead productive lives and have the freedom to enjoy the fruits of their labors.

> *They will build houses and dwell in them; they will plant vineyards and eat their fruit.* –Ezekiel 65:21

There are provisions made for the rights of families.

> *You are to allot it as an inheritance for yourselves and for the aliens who have settled among you and who have children.*
> –Ezekiel 47:22

17. Freedom of Religion - There will be only one established state religion. Embracing any other religion that doesn't involve worshipping the Lord and King will be considered an act of rebellion and will be met with swift punishment.

> *All kings will bow down to him and all nations will serve him.*
> –Psalm 72:11

> *If any of the peoples of the earth do not go up to Jerusalem to worship the King, the Lord Almighty, they will have no rain.*
> –Zechariah 14:17

> *"From one New Moon to another and from one Sabbath to another, all mankind will come and bow down before me," says the Lord.*
> –Isaiah 66:23
>
> *On that day there will be one Lord, and his name the only name.*
> –Zechariah 14:9

18. Freedom of Speech - Much of what we consider to be freedom of speech today will be voluntarily shut down when people behold and understand the greatness of the Lord and the power of his reign.

> *So will he sprinkle many nations, and kings will shut their mouths because of him. For what they were not told, they will see, and what they have not heard, they will understand.* –Isaiah 52:15

Others will be forced into silence.

> *Do you rulers indeed speak justly? . . . Break the teeth in their mouths, O God; tear out, O Lord, the fangs of the lions! Let them vanish like water that flows away . . . the righteous will be glad when they are avenged, when they bathe their feet in the blood of the wicked. The men will say, "Surely the righteous still are rewarded; surely there is a God who judges the earth."* –Psalm 58:1, 5, 10, 11

19. Freedom to Petition the Government - People will be able to bring grievances to the Lord, and his judges will hear their cases.

> *In any dispute, the priests are to serve as judges and decide it according to my ordinances.* –Ezekiel 44:24

20. Foreign Policy - The Lord's foreign policy, once his kingdom is established, is very simple. There are two basic options presented to the nations: 1) obey and receive rain which will empower your nation to trade, prosper and participate in activities in Jerusalem; 2) rebel and receive no rain which will result in famine, plague, economic failure and the ultimate collapse.

> *If any of the peoples of the earth do not go up to Jerusalem to worship the King, the Lord Almighty, they will have no rain.* –Zechariah 14:17

21. Gay Rights – The term "gay rights" is a kingdom oxymoron. There are no kingdom rights for those who live in rebellion to the king. Note the earlier descriptions of the king's treatment of rebels. Homosexuals will not be heirs in the kingdom, neither will male prostitutes nor any others who have lived in rebellion to the king during his absence from earth.

> *Do you not know that the wicked will not inherit the kingdom of God? Do not be deceived: Neither the sexually immoral nor idolaters nor*

adulterers nor male prostitutes nor homosexual offenders nor thieves nor the greedy nor drunkards nor slanderers nor swindlers will inherit the kingdom of God. –I Corinthians 6:9, 10

22. Global Presence - This is one of the key points of the Lord's political platform. The King and his kingdom will have a total global presence. There has never been an attempt to gloss over or disguise the Lord's intention of empire building across the globe. His advancement across the globe will continue until the entire world is under his jurisdiction.

> *The kingdom of the world has become the kingdom of our Lord and of his Christ, and he will reign forever and ever.* –Revelation 11:15

> *He will rule from sea to sea and from the River (Euphrates) to the ends of the earth.* –Psalm 72:8

23. Global Warming - The Lord's political policy does not have a plan to reduce global warming. It appears that under his administration the Lord himself turns up the heat, or at least, the amount of sunlight.

> *The moon will shine like the sun, and the sunlight will be seven times brighter, like the light of seven full days.* –Isaiah 30:26

24. Government Reform - The Lord's political platform supports and will implement what we might call Complete Universal Government Reform. In this model all current government officials in enemy nations are removed (and most likely executed) then replaced with individuals selected by the Lord and King himself.

> *To him who overcomes and does my will to the end, I will give authority over the nations—"He will rule them with an iron scepter; he will dash them to pieces like pottery"—just as I have received authority from my Father.* –Revelation 2:26, 27

> *I saw thrones on which were seated those who had been given authority to judge. And I saw the souls of those who had been beheaded because of their testimony for Jesus and because of the word of God . . . They came to life and reigned with Christ a thousand years.* –Revelation 20:4

> *On his robe and on his thigh he has this name written: KING OF KINGS AND LORD OF LORDS.* –Revelation 19:16

The other kings and lords mentioned in the verse above are the members of the Lord's new government. They are those appointed to rule with him, for him and under him as he rebuilds the governments of the world. They will rule with Christ in his administration of the iron scepter, dashing rebels like pottery.

> *To him who overcomes and does my will to the end, I will give authority over the nations—"He will rule them with an iron scepter; he will dash them to pieces like pottery"—just as I have received authority from my Father.* –Revelation 2:26, 27

25. Health Care - The alterations in topography that result in a dramatic increase in agricultural production will pave the way for new medical discoveries.

> *Fruit trees of all kinds will grow on both banks of the river. Their leaves will not wither, nor will their fruit fail . . . Their fruit will serve for food and their leaves for healing.* –Ezekiel 47:12

Of course, upon the Lord's return, many of those needing health care will no longer require it.

> *Be strong, do not fear; your God will come, he will come with vengeance; with divine retribution he will come to save you. Then will the eyes of the blind be opened and the ears of the deaf unstopped. Then will the lame leap like a deer, and the mute tongue shout for joy.*
> –Isaiah 35:4-5

26. Immigration - Within the empire, various nations will have boundaries and people will have citizenship within those boundaries. People will be able to change their citizenship to a different nation within the kingdom. When they do switch they will be considered full citizens of the new nation they have chosen.

> *You are to allot it (the land) as an inheritance for yourselves and for the aliens who have settled among you and who have children. You are to consider them as native-born Israelites; along with you they are to be allotted an inheritance among the tribes of Israel. In whatever tribe the alien settles, there you are to give him his inheritance.* –Ezekiel 47:22-23

Notice there is legal documentation for alien land rights. It is not likely that a country will be invaded by another country because that would be considered a declaration of war, and the King does not permit war. Therefore, undocumented migration would likely not be tolerated. If it were to happen, we could assume that the invading country would receive no rain and, through a series of plagues and economic turmoil, cease to exist if they did not come back in line with the King's political platform (Zechariah 14:16-19).

27. Infrastructure - The Lord will build highways for people to come to Jerusalem. First there will be a highway built for the exiles of Israel to return to Israel on.

42   Chapter 4   The Policies of the Lord's Administration

> The Lord will dry up the gulf of the Egyptian sea; with a scorching wind he will sweep his hand over the Euphrates River. He will break it up into seven streams so that men can cross over in sandals. There will be a highway for the remnant of his people that is left from Assyria. –Isaiah 11:16

There will also be a highway built to accommodate the travelers to Jerusalem who have come to meet with the Lord for educational purposes:

> And a highway will be there; it will be called the Way of Holiness. The unclean will not journey on it; it will be for those who walk in that Way; wicked fools will not go about on it. No lion will be there, nor will any ferocious beast get up on it; they will not be found there. But only the redeemed will walk there, and the ransomed of the Lord will return. They will enter Zion with singing; everlasting joy will crown their heads. Gladness and joy will overtake them, and sorrow and sighing will flee away. –Isaiah 35:8-10

There will be a highway built for the nations traveling from the north (Assyria) and the south (Egypt) to Jerusalem for worship. This highway will also serve as a means of international travel.

> In that day there will be a highway from Egypt to Assyria. The Assyrians will go to Egypt and the Egyptians to Assyria. The Egyptians and Assyrians will worship together. –Isaiah 19:23-24

The city of Jerusalem will be zoned for temple services and residential areas. There will be specific districts where the priests and Levites will live.

> In the sacred district, measure off a section 25,000 cubits long and 10,000 cubits wide. In it will be the sanctuary, the Most Holy Place. It will be the sacred portion of the land for the priests, who minister in the sanctuary and who draw near to minister before the Lord. It will be a place for their houses as well as a holy place for the sanctuary. An area 25,000 cubits long and 10,000 cubits wide will belong to the Levites, who serve in the temple, as their possession for towns to live in. You are to give the city as its property an area 5,000 cubits wide and 25,0000 cubits long, adjoining the sacred portion; it will belong to the whole house of Israel. –Ezekiel 45:3-6

There will be zoning laws for land set apart for farming, pasture and residential development.

> The remaining area, 5,000 cubits wide and 25,000 cubits long, will be for the common use of the city, for houses and for pastureland . . . The pastureland for the city will be 250 cubits on the north, 250 cubits on the south, 250 cubits on the east, and 250 cubits on the west. What remains of the area, bordering on the sacred portion and running the

length of it, will be 10,000 cubits on the east side and 10,000 cubits on the west side. Its produce will supply food for the workers of the city. – Ezekiel 48:15, 17, 18

There is an incredible public worship center (Ezekiel 40-47) designed to accommodate the arrival, departure and travel of people coming to worship in Jerusalem.

> When the people of the land come before the Lord at the appointed feasts, whoever enters by the north gate to worship is to go out the south gate, and whoever enters by the south gate is to go out the north gate. No one is to return through the gate by which he entered, but each is to go out the opposite gate. –Ezekiel 46:9-10

28. International Relationships - The Lord will be the international judge as well as the international king. Any conflicts that arise between nations will not be resolved through negotiations, peace treaties or military activity. All international crises will be resolved by the Judge in Jerusalem.

> He will judge between the nations and will settle disputes for many people. –Isaiah 2:4

Nations will grow to love the Lord along with Israel. They will desire to learn from him, live with him in his kingdom and worship him in his glory. The international community will unite itself under the Lord's reign.

> In that day Israel will be the third, along with Egypt and Assyria, a blessing on the earth. The Lord Almighty will bless them, saying, "Blessed be Egypt my people, Assyria my handiwork, and Israel my inheritance." –Isaiah 19:24, 25

> In that day a great trumpet will sound. Those who were perishing in Assyria and those who were exiled in Egypt will come and worship the Lord on the holy mountain in Jerusalem. –Isaiah 27:13

29. Israel and the Land – Upon his return, the Lord's Middle East policy is completely pro-Israel. Of course, Israel has been under the Lord's discipline and training for some 2,000 years (plus seven more years of intense pressure) leading them to consider and accept Jesus Christ as their Lord and King. When Jesus does return this is how he will treat Israel and how he will divide the land currently called "Palestine" by the Gentiles:

> "I will take the Israelites out of the nations where they have gone. I will gather them from all around and bring them back into their own land. I will make them one nation in the land on the mountains of Israel . . . My servant David will be king over them, and they will all have one shepherd . . . They and their children and their children's children will live there forever, and David my servant will be their prince forever .

Chapter 4 The Policies of the Lord's Administration

> . . I will make a covenant of peace with them . . . I will establish them and increase their numbers . . . My dwelling place will be with them . . . then the nations will know that I the Lord make Israel holy, when my sanctuary is among them forever." –Ezekiel 38:24-28

> In that day the Lord will reach out his hand a second time to reclaim the remnant that is left of his people from Assyria, from Lower Egypt, from Upper Egypt, from Cush, from Elam, from Babylonia, from Hamath and from the islands of the sea. He will raise a banner for the nations and gather the exiles of Israel; he will assemble the scattered people of Judah from the four quarters of the earth . . . Judah's enemies will be cut off . . . The Lord will dry up the gulf of the Egyptian sea; with a scorching wind he will sweep his hand over the Euphrates River. He will break it up into seven streams so that men can cross over in sandals. There will be a highway for the remnant of his people that is left from Assyria, as there was for Israel when they came up from Egypt.
> –Isaiah 11:12-16

30. Jobs - All the jobs required for a normal society to operate will continue during the Lord's kingdom on earth, but those jobs will be performed at a very high level in an economy with very high production, consumption and expansion. Labor will not be performed in vain; it will not be unproductive.

> They will not toil in vain. –Isaiah 65:23

There will be extensive government projects that employ many of the citizens of the king's realm, such as highway construction (Isaiah 11:6; 19:23; 35:8) and the construction of an extensive worship center in Jerusalem (Ezekiel 40-42).

The priest and Levites will be employed at public expense. Other jobs specifically mentioned are fishing (Ezekiel 47:9-11), farming (Ezekiel 48:19), residential construction (Isaiah 65:21), medical research (Ezekiel 47:12), and the tending of trees and their fruit (Ezekiel 47:12). There will be six days of work each week during which time the gate of the inner court facing east must be kept shut.

> The gate of the inner court facing east is to be shut on the six working days, but on the Sabbath day and on the day of the New Moon it is to be opened. –Ezekiel 46:2

31. Private Property - The Lord and King will encourage the ownership of private property and, specifically, the ownership of land by the citizens

> The prince must not take any of the inheritance of the people, driving them off their property. –Ezekiel 46:18

The Political Platform of the Lord and King

My princes will no longer oppress my people but will allow the house of Israel to possess the land according to their tribes. –Ezekiel 45:8

32. Race Relations - The Lord's kingdom will be known for its rich diversity of races, languages, tribes and nations. Although in this kingdom there will be various races and nations, this diversity will not be a source of division since in Christ there is neither Jew nor Greek. The unifying factor will be faith in Jesus Christ as Savior and Lord.

> *I looked and there before me was a great multitude that no one could count, from every nation, tribe, people and language, standing before the throne and in front of the Lamb.* –Revelation 7:9

> *There is neither Jew nor Greek, slave nor free, male nor female, for you are all one in Christ Jesus.* –Galatians 3:28

Concerning racial profiling, the people in the Lord's kingdom will be profiled not by the color of their skin, but by their relationship with the King. Believers in Jesus Christ have been made Sons of God and have been given the keys to the Kingdom. Those who are not believers will be profiled as unbelievers and removed. Race will not be an issue. Only faith in Christ will be of concern.

33. Social Justice - The Lord will be the judge. He will hear and decide cases for people who have come to him seeking justice.

> *He will not judge by what he sees with his eyes, or decide by what he hears with his ears; but with righteousness he will judge the needy, with justice he will give decisions for the poor of the earth.*
> –Isaiah 11:3-4

Each nation and its culture will benefit from the Lord's justice and will be blessed by it. No nation will be neglected by his administration.

> *All nations will be blessed through him, and they will call him blessed.*
> –Psalm 72:17

34. Taxation - The nations conquered by the Lord will bring him tribute. If they do not, they will be punished.

> *The desert tribes will bow before him and his enemies will lick the dust. The kings of Tarshish and of distant shores will bring tribute to him; the kings of Sheba and Seba will present him gifts. All kings will bow down to him and all nations will serve him.* –Psalm 72:9, 10

All the people are to provide him a special gift of wheat, barely and oil, plus one out of every 200 sheep (Ezekiel 45:13).

35. Unions - The priests and Levites will have union benefits in the sense that no one else can be employed in temple worship and sacrifices and offerings. Yet, it does not appear they will be negotiating their contracts or going on strike without facing the wrath of the One who rules with an iron scepter.

> These are the sons of Zadok, who are the only Levites who may draw near to the Lord to minister before him. –Ezekiel 40:46

36. Values - The Lord knows that right living produces the good things that mankind desires in life. The political platform of the Lord will be based on justice and righteousness. His administration will reflect these values and the people of the kingdom will be held to this standard. This will result in what the world has been seeking for a very long time: peace, quiet and confidence.

> Justice will dwell in the desert and righteousness live in the fertile field. The fruit of righteousness will be peace; the effect of righteousness will be quietness and confidence forever.
> –Isaiah 32:16-17

37. Welfare - The Lord's political platform takes a strong stance when it comes to helping the underprivileged, weak and poor. But one thing that stands out as part of this platform is the Lord's intention to assist them so they need no longer be underprivileged, weak or poor. When the Lord helps someone, he fully expects his efforts to be fruitful. The Lord's governmental assistance will not leave the needy in their state of need. The aid provided by the government will put them in a position to be contributing members of the Lord's kingdom. His program will abolish the welfare state by truly helping people instead of enabling them to remain dependent.

> In that day I will gather the lame; I will assemble the exiles and those I have brought to grief. I will make the lame a remnant, those driven away a strong nation. The Lord will rule over them in Mount Zion from that day and forever. –Micah 5:7

> I will lead the blind by ways they have not known, along unfamiliar paths I will guide them; I will turn the darkness into light before them and make the rough places smooth. These are the things I will do; I will not forsake them. –Isaiah 42:16, 17

> He will judge your people in righteousness, your afflicted ones with justice. –Psalm 72:2

> He will deliver the needy who cry out, the afflicted who have no one to help. He will take pity on the weak and the needy and save the needy from death. He will rescue them from oppression and violence. –Psalm 72:12-14

The poor and the needy will be a concern for the Lord in his kingdom. They will be treated fairly with righteousness and justice. They will not be accommodated simply because they are poor; they will be evaluated with righteous judgment and responded to with justice.

> *With righteousness he will judge the needy, with justice he will give decisions for the poor of the earth.* –Isaiah 11:4

Chapter Five
The Final Battle

When the Lord sets up his empire on earth over the nations of the world, the only citizens initially will be believers. Only those who have sided with the Lord will be allowed to enter his kingdom. Non-believers will be removed from the earth. These citizens who live in the kingdom of the Lord will come from one of two places. They will have either returned to earth with the Lord from heaven or they will still be alive on earth at the Lord's return to the Mount of Olives. Believers who have died before the Lord's return will come back with him.

> *Then the Lord my God will come, and all the holy ones with him.*
> –Zechariah 14:5

> *See, the Lord is coming with thousands upon thousands of his holy ones to judge everyone, and to convict all the ungodly of all the ungodly acts they have done in the ungodly way, and of all the harsh words ungodly sinners have spoken against him.* –Jude 14-15

> *Fine linen, bright and clean, was given her to wear. Fine linen stands for the righteous acts of the saints . . . He is dressed in a robe dipped in blood, and his name is the Word of God. The armies of heaven were following him, riding on white horses and dressed in fine linen, white and clean.* –Revelation 19:8, 13, 14

Indeed, the armies of heaven that return with Jesus will include the angels of God (2 Thessalonians 1:7), but they will also include the resurrected dead (Revelation 2:26, 27).

Those who are still living on the earth are the sheep who will have passed successfully through the sheep and goat judgment (Matthew 25:31-46). These "sheep" or believers will not die, but will continue to live their lives under the rule of the new administration. The "goats" or unbelievers who demonstrated their lack of faith by their actions will be removed from the earth and will not be part of the kingdom of the Lord and King.

> *When the Son of Man comes in his glory, and all the angels with him, he will sit on his throne in heavenly glory. All the nations will be gathered before him and he will separate the people one from another as a shepherd separates the sheep from the goats. He will put the sheep on his right and the goats on his left. Then the King will say to those on his right, "Come, you who are blessed by my Father; take your inheritance, the kingdom prepared for you since the creation of the world."* –Matthew 25:31-34

> *That is how it will be at the coming of the Son of Man. Two men will be in the field; one will be taken and the other left. Two women will be*

> grinding with a hand mill; one will be taken and the other left.
> –Matthew 24:39-41

In the above verse, the people who are left behind on the earth will enter the kingdom. This is not a verse referring to the rapture because it is in the context of Jesus' second coming. It is also found in the book of Matthew—a book which addresses the Jews and not the church. The ones who are taken are not taken to heaven, because the Lord has just come to from heaven to earth. The ones who are taken are the goats spoken of in Matthew 25:31-46. They are removed from the earth and sent to eternal punishment (Matthew 25:41, 46). Hear the words of the King:

> He will put the sheep on his right and the goats on his left . . . Then he will say to those on his left, "Depart from me, you who are cursed, into the eternal fire prepared for the devil and his angels" . . . Then they will go away to eternal punishment. –Matthew 25:33, 41, 46

The political platform of the Lord and King will be set up in a kingdom that is initially made up entirely of believers who are willingly obedient to the King's rule. The resurrected saints from all of time who returned with the Lord will live in the kingdom and assist in its administration. The people who were living on earth at the Lord's return will enter the kingdom after the sheep and goat judgment. These people will return to their home nations to continue living their earthly lives under the authority and blessing of the Lord's empire. These people will marry, have children and raise families in this new age.

> This is what the Lord says: "I will return to Zion and dwell in Jerusalem. Then Jerusalem will be called the City of Truth, and the mountain of the Lord Almighty will be called the Holy Mountain." This is what the Lord Almighty says: "Once again men and women of ripe old age will sit in the streets of Jerusalem, each with cane in hand because of his age. The city streets will be filled with boys and girls playing there." –Zechariah 8:3-5

> "Never again will there be in it an infant who lives but a few days, or an old man who does not live out his years; he who dies at a hundred will be thought a mere youth; he who fails to reach a hundred will be considered accursed. They will build houses and dwell in them; they will plant vineyards and eat their fruit. No longer will they build houses and others live in them, or plant and others eat. For as the days of a tree, so will be the days of my people; my chosen ones will long enjoy the works of their hands. They will not toil in vain or bear children doomed to misfortune; for they will be a people blessed by the Lord, they and their descendants with them. Before they call I will answer; while they are still speaking I will hear. The wolf and the lamb will feed together, and the lion will eat straw like the ox, but dust will be the serpent's food. They will neither harm nor destroy on all my holy mountain," says the Lord. –Isaiah 65:20-25

Chapter 5 **The Final Battle**

> *You are to allot it as an inheritance for yourselves and for the aliens who have settled among you and who have children. You are to consider them as native-born Israelites; along with you they are to be allotted an inheritance among the tribes of Israel. In whatever tribe the alien settles, there you are to give him his inheritance.*
> –Ezekiel 47:22-23

The Lord will reign over the earth year after year. Centuries will pass as the Lord's kingdom far exceeds the previous world empires of Egypt, Assyria, Babylon, Persia, Greece, Rome, etc. It will be an age of extreme prosperity. Nature will be restored. Businesses will thrive. International peace will be enforced. Courts will be fair and just. It will be a golden age of righteousness. But, it will not be without challenges. The Lord and King will navigate his way through any difficulties that arise with wisdom and justice.

As soon as the golden age begins, the citizens of the kingdom who came from the conquered nations will start to have children. These children will have free will. With his or her own volition, each person will be free to accept or reject the rule of the King. Even though the King is flawless in his reign and the empire is overflowing with peace and prosperity, many will not want to submit to his grace and blessing. There will be times of rebellion in the Lord and King's empire, but in strength, wisdom, righteousness and justice the Lord will quickly quench and punish all revolt.

> *Then the survivors from all the nations that have attacked Jerusalem will go up year after year to worship the King, the Lord Almighty, and to celebrate the Feast of Tabernacles. If any of the peoples of the earth do not go up to Jerusalem to worship the King, the Lord Almighty, they will nave no rain. . . .The Lord will bring on them the plague he inflicts on the nation that do not go up to celebrate the Feast of Tabernacles.*
> –Zechariah 14:16-19

After a one thousand year reign, the Lord will allow Satan to be released back onto the earth to test and deceive the members of the kingdom who have harbored rebellion in their hearts. This will result in a worldwide rebellion of the nations again. Nations will march on Jerusalem in an attempt to dethrone the Lord and King—culminating in a swift and final judgment. Fire from heaven will consume the insurgents.

> *When the thousand years are over, Satan will be released from his prison and will go out to deceive the nations in the four corners of the earth – God and Magog – to gather them for battle. In number they are like the sand on the seashore. They marched across the breadth of the earth and surrounded the camp of God's people, the city he loves. But fire came down from heaven and devoured them. And the devil, who deceived them, was thrown into the lake of burning sulfur . . .*
> –Revelation 20:7-10

These events will be signs that the end of this physical earth is near. But the kingdom of the Lord will continue forever in a new universe created for the eternal reign of Jesus Christ the King.

> *The day of the Lord will come like a thief. The heavens will disappear with a roar; the elements will be destroyed by fire, and the earth and everything in it will be laid bare . . . That day will bring about the destruction of the heavens by fire, and the elements will melt in the heat. But in keeping with his promise we are looking forward to a new heaven and a new earth, the home of righteousness.* –II Peter 3:10-13

The destruction of the universe will be followed by the final judgment of all the wicked who have died throughout time.

> *Then I saw a great white throne and him who was seated on it. Earth and sky fled from his presence, and there was not place for them. And I saw the dead, great and small, standing before the throne, and books were opened. Another book was opened, which is the book of life. The dead were judged according to what they had done as recorded in the books. The sea gave up the dead that were in it and death and Hades gave up the dead that were in them, and each person was judged according to what he had done. Then death and Hades were thrown into the lake of fire. The lake of fire is the second death. If anyone's name was not found written in the book of life, he was thrown into the lake of fire.* –Revelation 20:11-15

This is the judgment that includes the "goats" who had been removed during the sheep and goat judgment, but it also includes non-believers from all time who had been waiting in Hades. Once this judgment of all unbelievers is complete, Hades itself is thrown into Hell, or the Lake of Fire.

After this the Lord and King Jesus Christ will submit his eternal kingdom to God the Father in preparation for eternity in a New Heaven and New Earth.

Chapter Six
The Transfer of the Empire

The Lord Jesus Christ will rule the earth and his kingdom will never end. But, there will come a day when he hands the kingdom over to the Father. Paul describes this in I Corinthians:

> Then the end will come, when he hands over the kingdom to God the Father after he has destroyed all dominion, authority and power. For he must reign until he has put all his enemies under his feet. The last enemy to be destroyed is death. For he "has put everything under his feet." –I Corinthians 15:24-27

The Lord and King will continue to rule on the earth until he has destroyed all dominion, authority and power. The Lord will destroy the authority of the nations when he returns to the Mount of Olives. He will then rule and reign as King of the earth for a thousand years. During this time the Lord and King will put down any revolt by any enemy and any conspiracy by any dominion coming against his political platform. After a successful one thousand year rule, the Lord will face Satan for a final showdown to demonstrate and secure the Lord's complete dominion in time over every power in heaven and on earth. This is followed by the final judgment of fallen man and the removal of death itself into the Lake of Fire.

> Then death and Hades were thrown into the Lake of Fire. –Revelation 20:14

Jesus will reign until he has conquered every enemy of God including the nations, Satan, and death (There will be death in the kingdom, see "Death Penalty"). After the Lord and King has subdued all opposition, his eternal kingdom will continue forever under the headship of God the Father. Jesus Christ will hand his kingdom over to God. In this arrangement, the Lord and King will continue to rule as God the Father continues to extend his authority to Jesus Christ forever and ever. (I Corinthians 15:24-27)

So that the plan of God will continue, God will create a new heaven and earth—a new universe. Isaiah spoke of this new state in a passage where he also described the reign of the Lord and King on the old earth.

> Behold, I will create a new heaven and a new earth. The former things will not be remembered, nor will they come to mind. But be glad and rejoice forever in what I create, for I will create Jerusalem to be a delight and its people a joy. I will rejoice over Jerusalem and take delight in my people; the sound of weeping and of crying will be heard in it no more. –Isaiah 65:17

> Then I saw a new heaven and a new earth, for the first heaven and the first earth had passed away, and there was no longer any sea. –Revelation 21:1

In this new earth, the city of God, or heaven itself, will come to dwell on the earth with man. This eternal city of God, not built with human hands, is called "The New Jerusalem."

> *I saw the Holy City, the new Jerusalem, coming down out of heaven from God, prepared as a bride beautifully dressed for her husband. And I heard a loud voice from the throne saying, "Now the dwelling of God is with men, and he will live with them. They will be his people, and God himself will be with them and be their God. He will wipe every tear from their eyes. There will be no more death or mourning or crying or pain, for the old order of things has passed away.* –Revelation 21:2-4

This new Jerusalem that is prepared like a bride is Heaven itself. It is the city Abraham longed to see, the home of the presence and throne of God the Father. It is an eternal city not built by human hands. (Just because the Holy City is compared to a "bride" does not mean the new Jerusalem is the church. The new Jerusalem is the Holy City. The church is not the Holy City. The presence of a new Jerusalem on earth brings God's dwelling place to men. To be the church means you already have God's presence living inside you. We, the church, are not bringing God's presence to ourselves in this new heaven and new earth.) Again, this is the city that Abraham was looking for.

> *For he (Abraham) was looking forward to the city with foundations, whose architect and builder is God.* –Hebrews 11:10

Later in the book of Hebrews, this city of the living God is called "heavenly Jerusalem" and "Mount Zion." It is identified as the place for angels, the church, God, the spirits of righteous men and Jesus. The new Jerusalem is heaven, the very home of God, that has come to a new earth in a new universe.

> *You have come to Mount Zion, to the heavenly Jerusalem, the city of the living God. You have come to thousands upon thousands of angels in joyful assembly, to the church of the firstborn, whose names are written in heaven. You have come to God, the judge of all men, to the spirits of righteous men made perfect, to Jesus the mediator of a new covenant, and to the sprinkled blood that speaks a better word than the blood of Abel."* –Hebrews 12:22-24

This new earth is created in order to sustain the eternal kingdom of Jesus Christ. Think of it as a new baseball stadium. If a baseball team is performing poorly and attendance is always down, an old park will do just fine for many, many years. But, if new management takes over and the policies are changed for the better, things begin to happen. The players start to perform better, championships are won, attendance goes up and parking becomes a problem. Soon the old stadium cannot sustain the growth and production prompted by the new policies. The old stadium is actually holding back the new administration from even greater things. It is time to not just refurbish the old stadium, but to build a new stadium

Chapter 6 **The Transfer of the Empire**

that can accommodate the vast improvements the new management has brought to the franchise. In this new earth, the kingdom of the Lord Jesus Christ will continue forever and ever, outperforming anything that could be accomplished in the old earth.

Welcome to the eternal state!

> *He who was seated on the throne said, "I am making everything new!" Then he said, "Write this down, for these words are trustworthy and true." He said to me, "It is done. I am the Alpha and the Omega, the Beginning and the End. To him who is thirsty I will give to drink without cost from the spring of the water of life. He who overcomes will inherit all this, and I will be his God and he will be my son. But the cowardly, the unbelieving, the vile, the murderers, the sexually immoral, those who practice magic arts, the idolaters and all liars—their place will be in the fiery lake of burning sulfur. This is the second death." One of the seven angels who had the seven bowls full of the seven last plagues came and said to me, "Come, I will show you the bride, the wife of the Lamb." And he carried me away in the Spirit to a mountain great and high, and showed me the Holy City, Jerusalem, coming down out of heaven from God. It shone with the glory of God, and its brilliance was like that of a very precious jewel, like a jasper, clear as crystal. It had a great, high wall with twelve gates, and with twelve angels at the gates. On the gates were written the names of the twelve tribes of Israel. There were three gates on the east, three on the north, three on the south and three on the west. The wall of the city had twelve foundations, and on them were the names of the twelve apostles of the Lamb. The angel who talked with me had a measuring rod of gold to measure the city, its gates and its walls. The city was laid out like a square, as long as it was wide. He measured the city with the rod and found it to be 12,000 stadia in length, and as wide and high as it is long. He measured its wall and it was 144 cubits thick, by man's measurement, which the angel was using. The wall was made of jasper, and the city of pure gold, as pure as glass. The foundations of the city walls were decorated with every kind of precious stone. The first foundation was jasper, the second sapphire, the third chalcedony, the fourth emerald, the fifth sardonyx, the sixth carnelian, the seventh chrysolite, the eighth beryl, the ninth topaz, the tenth chrysoprase, the eleventh jacinth, and the twelfth amethyst. The twelve gates were twelve pearls, each gate made of a single pearl. The great street of the city was of pure gold, like transparent glass. I did not see a temple in the city, because the Lord God Almighty and the Lamb are its temple. The city does not need the sun or the moon to shine on it, for the glory of God gives it light, and the Lamb is its lamp. The nations will walk by its light, and the kings of the earth will bring their splendor into it. On no day will its gates ever be shut, for there will be no night there. The glory and honor of the nations will be brought into it. Nothing impure will ever enter it, nor will anyone who does what is shameful or deceitful, but only those whose names are written in the Lamb's book of life.* –Revelation 21:5-27

Chapter Seven
Meeting the Lord and King Today

We are not living on a new earth today, nor are we are living under the reign of the Lord and King in his kingdom. We are living in an age where Jesus is still calling people, through the Holy Spirit and the church, to come to him.

> *The Spirit and the bride say, "Come!" And let him who hears say, "Come!" Whoever is thirsty, let him come, and whoever wishes let him take the free gift of the water of life.* –Revelation 22:17

Today is the day of salvation. Today is the day of grace. Today is a day to come to God through faith in Jesus Christ and his death on the cross. Jesus Christ will come as the Lord and King to rule and reign. When he physically returns to this planet, it will be too late. The offer of citizenship in his kingdom will be closed upon his return. But today you can place your faith in him. You can trust the King who died for your sins on the cross.

> *Salvation is found in no one else, for there is no other name under heaven given to men by which we must be saved.* –Acts 4:12

This is what the Lord says—Israel's King and Redeemer, the Lord Almighty:
I am the first and I am the last;
 apart from me there is no God.
Who then is like me?
Let him proclaim it.
Let him declare and lay out before me what has happened since I established my ancient people, and what is yet to come - yes, let him foretell what will come.
Do not tremble, do not be afraid.
Did I not proclaim this and foretell it long ago?
You are my witnesses.
Is there any God besides me?
No, there is no other Rock; I know not one . . .
I am the Lord, who has made all things,
who alone stretched out the heavens,
who spread out the earth by myself,
who foils the signs of false prophets and makes fools of diviners,
who overthrows the learning of the wise and turns it into nonsense,
who carries out the words of his servants and
fulfills the predictions of his messengers,
who says of Jerusalem, "It shall be inhabited,"
of the towns of Judah, "They shall be built."
–Isaiah 44:6-8; 24-26

Chapter 7 Meeting the Lord and King Today

In love a throne will be established; in faithfulness a man will sit on it—one from the house of David—one who in judging seeks justice and speeds the cause of righteousness. –Isaiah 16:5

He must remain in heaven until the time comes for God to restore everything, as he promised long ago through his holy prophets.
–Acts 3:21

*YOUR KINGDOM COME, YOUR WILL BE DONE
ON EARTH AS IT IS IN HEAVEN.* –Matthew 6:10

This gospel of the kingdom will be preached in the whole world as a testimony to all nations, and then the end will come. –Matthew 24:14